**6.** Enter your class ID code to join a class.

### YOU HAVE A CLASS ID CODE FROM YOUR TEACHER

**a.** Enter your class code and click

Next

**b.** Students in a class can use the Discussion Board and Email tools.

**c.** To enter the class ID code later, choose **Join a Class**.

Join a Class

### YOU DO NOT HAVE A CLASS ID CODE

**a.** You do not need a class ID code to use *iQ Online*. Click

Skip

**b.** To enter the class ID code later, choose **Join a Class**.

Join a Class

**7.** Check your registration information and click Log In. Then choose your book. Click **Activities** to begin using *iQ Online*.

Activities

### IMPORTANT

- After you register, the next time you want to use *iQ Online*, go to www.iQOnlinePractice.com. Log in with your email address and password.

- You can use *iQ Online* for 12 months from the date you register.

- For help, please contact customer service: eltsupport@oup.com.

**OXFORD**
UNIVERSITY PRESS

198 Madison Avenue
New York, NY 10016 USA

Great Clarendon Street, Oxford, OX2 6DP, United Kingdom

Oxford University Press is a department of the University of Oxford.
It furthers the University's objective of excellence in research, scholarship,
and education by publishing worldwide. Oxford is a registered trade
mark of Oxford University Press in the UK and in certain other countries

Adult Content Director: Stephanie Karras
Publisher: Sharon Sargent
Managing Editor: Mariel DeKranis
Development Editor: Eric Zuarino
Head of Digital, Design, and Production: Bridget O'Lavin
Executive Art and Design Manager: Maj-Britt Hagsted
Design Project Manager: Debbie Lofaso
Content Production Manager: Julie Armstrong
Image Manager: Trisha Masterson
Image Editor: Liaht Ziskind
Production Coordinator: Brad Tucker

ISBN: 978 0 19 481807 0 Student Book intro with iQ Online pack
ISBN: 978 0 19 481808 7 Student Book intro as pack component
ISBN: 978 0 19 481802 5 iQ Online student website

Printed in China
This book is printed on paper from certified and well-managed sources.

ACKNOWLEDGEMENTS

*Illustrations by:* p. 5 Greg Paprocki; p. 17 Stacy Merlin; p. 23 Karen Minot;
p. 28 Stacy Merlin; p. 39 Greg Paprocki; p. 45 Stuart Bradford; p. 48 Barb
Bastian; p. 56 Karen Minot; p. 61 Stuart Bradford; p. 76 Karen Minot;
p. 87 Karen Minot; p. 90 Karen Minot; p. 98 Greg Paprocki; p. 125 Stacy
Merlin; p. 133 Stacy Merlin; p. 148 Stuart Bradford.

*We would also like to thank the following for permission to reproduce the following
photographs:* Cover: David Pu'u/Corbis; Video Vocabulary (used throughout
the book): Oleksiy Mark/Shutterstock; p. 2 Hero Images/Corbis;
p. 4 UpperCut Images/Alamy; p. 6 PhotoAlto/Alamy; p. 9 Paul Matzner/Alamy;
p. 12 SSPL/Science Museum/Getty Images; p. 15 David Pu'u/Corbis UK Ltd.;
p. 20 Blend Images/Ariel Skelley/Getty Images; p. 21 ZUMA Press, Inc./Alamy,
CollinsChin/Getty Images; p. 22 Rick Friedman/Corbis UK Ltd.; p. 25 Daniel
Teetor/Alamy; p. 27 PeopleImages.com/Getty Images; p. 31 Stephen
Shepherd/Alamy; p. 32 Peter Christopher/Masterfile/Masterfile Royalty Free;
p. 34 Bob Peterson/Getty Images; p. 36 Anthony Pidgeon/Getty Images;
p. 37 Ariel Skelley/Blend Images/Corbis, Yasonya/Shutterstock; p. 38 Adrianna
Williams/Corbis UK Ltd.; p. 39 Daly and Newton/Getty Images; p. 40 Fancy/
Alamy; p. 43 Photodisc/Oxford University Press; p. 44 G. Biss/Masterfile/
Masterfile Royalty Free; p. 47 Tim Hill/Alamy; p. 53 Joggie Botma/Alamy;
p. 54 Monkey Business Images/Monkey/Corbis UK Ltd.; p. 55 2008 AFP/Getty
Images (books), Adriano Castelli/Shutterstock (exhibition), Image Source/
Getty Images (path), Goodshoot/Thinkstock (crowded), Patrick Batchelder/
Alamy (architecture), Betsie Van Der Meer/Getty Images (outdoors), David
Lyons/Alamy (nature), Sam Edwards/Getty Images (relaxing); p. 56 Luís
Henrique Boucault/Getty Images (shopping), Absodels/Getty Images (judo); p. 60 Blue Jean Images/Alamy;
p. 63 Maridav/Shutterstock; p. 64 John Harper/Getty Images; p. 65 Christopher
Malcolm/Getty Images (basketball), Carolyn Clarke/Alamy (park); p. 66 Mint
Images Limited/Alamy (woman), Abel Mitja Varela/Getty Images (man);
p. 70 Xavier Arnau/Getty Images, gresei/Shutterstock; p. 71 Dann Tardif/
LWA/Corbis, Glow Images, Inc/Getty Images; p. 73 William Caram/Alamy
(houses), Yellow Dog Productions/Getty Images (dorm), PhotoStock-Israel/
Alamy (studio apartment), Stock Connection/Superstock Ltd. (large house);
p. 77 A. Astes/Alamy; p. 80 Kazuhiro Nogi/AFP/Getty Images (Dr. Chan), Aaron
Kohr/Shutterstock (for rent); p. 82 Russell Kord/Alamy; p. 83 Konstantin L/
Shutterstock; p. 85 Steve Heap/Shutterstock (pool), 13/Image Source/Ocean/
Corbis UK Ltd. (fireplace); p. 93 Henryk Sadura Tetra Images/Newscom;
p. 94 Klaus Mellenthin/Getty Images; p. 95 Marka/Superstock Ltd.
(sphygmomanometer), moodboard/Alamy (stressed); p. 101 Fuse/Getty
Images (salad), Zoonar GmbH/Alamy (excercise); p. 106 dboystudio/
Shutterstock; p. 107 Tetra Images/Alamy; p. 109 Mindscape studio/
Shutterstock; p. 114 Claire Takacs/Getty Images; p. 117 Japan Stock
Photography/Alamy (Kyoto), Charles E. Rotkin/Corbis UK Ltd. (Forum);
p. 118 Sylvain Sonnet/Getty Images (New York), Jones/Shimlock-Secret Sea
Visions/Getty Images (Ubud), Visions Of Our Land/Getty Images (Bruges), Matej
Pavlansky/Shutterstock (globe); p. 123 Photodisc/Oxford University Press
(blueprint), Portland Press Herald/Getty Images (meeting); p. 125 urbancow/
iStockphoto; p. 127 Lane Oatey/Blue Jean Images/Getty Images (architect),
Peter Adams/Getty Images (restaurant); p. 130 David Noton Photography/
Alamy; p. 131 Jack Hollingsworth/Alamy; p. 132 Goodshoot/Oxford
University Press (Acropolis), Hiroyuki Matsumoto/Getty Images (Mexico
City); p. 133 Travel Pictures Ltd/Superstock Ltd. (British Museum), Rudy
Sulgan/Corbis UK Ltd. (Nelson's Column), Photodisc/Oxford University Press
(Tower of London), Peter Phipp/Travelshots.com/Alamy (Shakespeare Globe);
p. 136 Eric Raptosh Photography/Blend Images/Corbis; p. 137 Zurijeta/
Shutterstock, Andy Dean Photography/Shutterstock, karamysh/
Shutterstock; p. 138 Colorsport/Corbis UK Ltd.; p. 139 Rubberball/
Rubberball/Corbis UK Ltd. (genius), Christophe Lehenaff/Getty Images
(astronomy); p. 140 Harvard College Observatory/Science Photo Library
(Henrietta Leavitt), Mike Agliolo/Corbis UK Ltd. (bulb); p. 143 Gary S
Chapman/Getty Images; p. 144 Ian Lishman/Juice Images/Corbis UK Ltd.;
p. 145 picsfive/Alamy (writing), epa/Corbis UK Ltd. (Naguib Mahfouz);
p. 149 Zurijeta/Shutterstock; p. 150 Juice Images/Alamy; p. 152 Juice Images/
Alamy (new car), Philipp Nemenz/Corbis UK Ltd. (phonecall); p. 154 Hadrian/
Shutterstock; p. 155 Atsushi Yamada/Getty Images; Back Cover: mozcann/
iStockphoto.

# SHAPING learning TOGETHER

We would like to acknowledge the teachers from all over the world who participated in the development process and review of the Q series.

## Special thanks to our Q: *Skills for Success* Second Edition Topic Advisory Board

**Shaker Ali Al-Mohammad**, Buraimi University College, Oman; **Dr. Asmaa A. Ebrahim**, University of Sharjah, U.A.E.; **Rachel Batchilder**, College of the North Atlantic, Qatar; **Anil Bayir**, Izmir University, Turkey; **Flora Mcvay Bozkurt**, Maltepe University, Turkey; **Paul Bradley**, University of the Thai Chamber of Commerce Bangkok, Thailand; **Joan Birrell-Bertrand**, University of Manitoba, MB, Canada; **Karen E. Caldwell**, Zayed University, U.A.E.; **Nicole Hammond Carrasquel**, University of Central Florida, FL, U.S.; **Kevin Countryman**, Seneca College of Applied Arts & Technology, ON, Canada; **Julie Crocker**, Arcadia University, NS, Canada; **Marc L. Cummings**, Jefferson Community and Technical College, KY, U.S.; **Rachel DeSanto**, Hillsborough Community College Dale Mabry Campus, FL, U.S.; **Nilüfer Ertürkmen**, Ege University, Turkey; **Sue Fine**, Ras Al Khaimah Women's College (HCT), U.A.E.; **Amina Al Hashami**, Nizwa College of Applied Sciences, Oman; **Stephan Johnson**, Nagoya Shoka Daigaku, Japan; **Sean Kim**, Avalon, South Korea; **Gregory King**, Chubu Daigaku, Japan; **Seran Küçük**, Maltepe University, Turkey; **Jonee De Leon**, VUS, Vietnam; **Carol Lowther**, Palomar College, CA, U.S.; **Erin Harris-MacLead**, St. Mary's University, NS, Canada; **Angela Nagy**, Maltepe University, Turkey; **Huynh Thi Ai Nguyen**, Vietnam; **Daniel L. Paller**, Kinjo Gakuin University, Japan; **Jangyo Parsons**, Kookmin University, South Korea; **Laila Al Qadhi**, Kuwait University, Kuwait; **Josh Rosenberger**, English Language Institute University of Montana, MT, U.S.; **Nancy Schoenfeld**, Kuwait University, Kuwait; **Jenay Seymour**, Hongik University, South Korea; **Moon-young Son**, South Korea; **Matthew Taylor**, Kinjo Gakuin Daigaku, Japan; **Burcu Tezcan-Unal**, Zayed University, U.A.E.; **Troy Tucker**, Edison State College-Lee Campus, FL, U.S.; **Kris Vicca**, Feng Chia University, Taichung; **Jisook Woo**, Incheon University, South Korea; **Dunya Yenidunya**, Ege University, Turkey

**UNITED STATES** Marcarena Aguilar, North Harris College, TX; Rebecca Andrade, California State University North Ridge, CA; Lesley Andrews, Boston University, MA; Deborah Anholt, Lewis and Clark College, OR; Robert Anzelde, Oakton Community College, IL; Arlys Arnold, University of Minnesota, MN; Marcia Arthur, Renton Technical College, WA; Renee Ashmeade, Passaic County Community College, NJ; Anne Bachmann, Clackamas Community College, OR; Lida Baker, UCLA, CA; Ron Balsamo, Santa Rosa Junior College, CA; Lori Barkley, Portland State University, OR; Eileen Barlow, SUNY Albany, NY; Sue Bartch, Cuyahoga Community College, OH; Lora Bates, Oakton High School, VA; Barbara Batra, Nassau County Community College, NY; Nancy Baum, University of Texas at Arlington, TX; Rebecca Beck, Irvine Valley College, CA; Linda Berendsen, Oakton Community College, IL; Jennifer Binckes Lee, Howard Community College, MD; Grace Bishop, Houston Community College, TX; Jean W. Bodman, Union County College, NJ; Virginia Bouchard, George Mason University, VA; Kimberley Briesch Sumner, University of Southern California, CA; Kevin Brown, University of California, Irvine, CA; Laura Brown, Glendale Community College, CA; Britta Burton, Mission College, CA; Allison L. Callahan, Harold Washington College, IL; Gabriela Cambiasso, Harold Washington College, IL; Jackie Campbell, Capistrano Unified School District, CA; Adele C. Camus, George Mason University, VA; Laura Chason, Savannah College, GA; Kerry Linder Catana, Language Studies International, NY; An Cheng, Oklahoma State University, OK; Carole Collins, North Hampton Community College, PA; Betty R. Compton, Intercultural Communications College, HI; Pamela Couch, Boston University, MA; Fernanda Crowe, Intrax International Institute, CA; Vicki Curtis, Santa Cruz, CA; Margo Czinski, Washtenaw Community College, MI; David Dahnke, Lone Star College, TX; Gillian M. Dale, CA; L. Dalgish, Concordia College, MN; Christopher Davis, John Jay College, NY; Sherry Davis, Irvine University, CA; Natalia de Cuba, Nassau County Community College, NY; Sonia Delgadillo, Sierra College, CA; Esmeralda Diriye, Cypress College & Cal Poly, CA; Marta O. Dmytrenko-Ahrabian, Wayne State University, MI; Javier Dominguez, Central High School, SC; Jo Ellen Downey-Greer, Lansing Community College, MI; Jennifer Duclos, Boston University, MA; Yvonne Duncan, City College of San Francisco, CA; Paul Dydman, USC Language Academy, CA; Anna Eddy, University of Michigan-Flint, MI; Zohan El-Gamal, Glendale Community College, CA; Jennie Farnell, University of Connecticut, CT; Susan Fedors, Howard Community College, MD; Valerie Fiechter, Mission College, CA; Ashley Fifer, Nassau County Community College, NY; Matthew Florence, Intrax International Institute, CA; Kathleen Flynn, Glendale College, CA; Elizabeth Fonsea, Nassau County Community College, NY; Eve Fonseca, St. Louis Community College, MO; Elizabeth Foss, Washtenaw Community College, MI; Duff C. Galda, Pima Community College, AZ; Christiane Galvani, Houston Community College, TX; Gretchen Gerber, Howard Community College, MD; Ray Gonzalez, Montgomery College, MD; Janet Goodwin, University of California, Los Angeles, CA; Alyona Gorokhova, Grossmont College, CA; John Graney, Santa Fe College, FL; Kathleen Green, Central High School, AZ; Nancy Hamadou, Pima Community College-West Campus, AZ; Webb Hamilton, De Anza College, San Jose City College, CA; Janet Harclerode, Santa Monica Community College, CA; Sandra Hartmann, Language and Culture Center, TX; Kathy Haven, Mission College, CA; Roberta Hendrick, Cuyahoga Community College, OH; Ginny Heringer, Pasadena City College, CA; Adam Henricksen, University of Maryland, MD; Carolyn Ho, Lone Star College-CyFair, TX; Peter Hoffman, LaGuardia Community College, NY; Linda Holden, College of Lake County, IL; Jana Holt, Lake Washington Technical College, WA; Antonio Iccarino, Boston University, MA; Gail Ibele, University of Wisconsin, WI; Nina Ito, American Language Institute, CSU Long Beach, CA; Linda Jensen, UCLA, CA; Lisa Jurkowitz, Pima Community College, CA; Mandy Kama, Georgetown University, Washington, DC; Stephanie Kasuboski, Cuyahoga Community College, OH; Chigusa Katoku, Mission College, CA; Sandra Kawamura, Sacramento City College, CA; Gail Kellersberger, University of Houston-Downtown, TX; Jane Kelly, Durham Technical Community College, NC; Maryanne Kildare, Nassau County Community College, NY; Julie Park Kim, George Mason University, VA; Kindra Kinyon, Los Angeles Trade-Technical College, CA; Matt Kline, El Camino College, CA; Lisa Kovacs-Morgan, University of California, San Diego, CA; Claudia Kupiec, DePaul University, IL; Renee La Rue, Lone Star College-Montgomery, TX; Janet Langon, Glendale College, CA; Lawrence Lawson, Palomar College, CA; Rachele Lawton, The Community College of Baltimore County, MD; Alice Lee, Richland College, TX; Esther S. Lee, CSUF & Mt. SAC, CA; Cherie Lenz-Hackett, University of Washington, WA; Joy Leventhal, Cuyahoga Community College, OH; Alice Lin, UCI Extension, CA; Monica Lopez, Cerritos College, CA; Dustin Lovell, FLS International Marymount College, CA; Carol Lowther, Palomar College, CA; Candace Lynch-Thompson, North Orange County Community College District, CA; Thi Thi Ma, City College of San Francisco, CA; Steve Mac Isaac, USC Long Academy, CA; Denise Maduli-Williams, City College of San Francisco, CA; Eileen Mahoney, Camelback High School, AZ; Naomi Mardock, MCC-Omaha, NE; Brigitte Maronde, Harold Washington College, IL; Marilyn Marquis, Laposita College CA; Doris Martin, Glendale Community College; Pasadena City College, CA; Keith Maurice, University of Texas at Arlington, TX; Nancy Mayer, University of Missouri-St. Louis, MO; Aziah McNamara, Kansas State University, KS; Billie McQuillan, Education Heights, MN; Karen Merritt, Glendale Union High School District, AZ; Holly Milkowart, Johnson County Community College, KS; Eric Moyer, Intrax International Institute, CA; Gino Muzzatti, Santa Rosa Junior College, CA; Sandra Navarro, Glendale Community College, CA; Than Nyeinkhin, ELAC, PCC, CA; William Nedrow, Triton College, IL; Eric Nelson, University of Minnesota, MN; Than Nyeinkhin, ELAC, PCC, CA; Fernanda Ortiz, Center for English as a Second Language at the University of Arizona, AZ; Rhony Ory, Ygnacio Valley High School, CA; Paul Parent, Montgomery College, MD; Dr. Sumeeta Patnaik, Marshall University, WV; Oscar Pedroso, Miami Dade College, FL; Robin Persiani, Sierra College, CA; Patricia Prenz-Belkin, Hostos Community College, NY; Suzanne Powell, University of Louisville, KY; Jim Ranalli, Iowa State University, IA; Toni R. Randall, Santa Monica College, CA; Vidya Rangachari, Mission College, CA; Elizabeth Rasmussen, Northern Virginia Community College, VA; Lara Ravitch, Truman College, IL;

Deborah Repasz, San Jacinto College, TX; Marisa Recinos, English Language Center, Brigham Young University, UT; Andrey Reznikov, Black Hills State University, SD; Alison Rice, Hunter College, NY; Jennifer Robles, Ventura Unified School District, CA; Priscilla Rocha, Clark County School District, NV; Dzidra Rodins, DePaul University, IL; Maria Rodriguez, Central High School, AZ; Josh Rosenberger, English Language Institute University of Montana, MT; Alice Rosso, Bucks County Community College, PA; Rita Rozzi, Xavier University, OH; Maria Ruiz, Victor Valley College, CA; Kimberly Russell, Clark College, WA; Stacy Sabraw, Michigan State University, MI; Irene Sakk, Northwestern University, IL; Deborah Sandstrom, University of Illinois at Chicago, IL; Jenni Santamaria, ABC Adult, CA; Shaeley Santiago, Ames High School, IA; Peg Sarosy, San Francisco State University, CA; Alice Savage, North Harris College, TX; Donna Schaeffer, University of Washington, WA; Karen Marsh Schaeffer, University of Utah, UT; Carol Schinger, Northern Virginia Community College, VA; Robert Scott, Kansas State University, KS; Suell Scott, Sheridan Technical Center, FL; Shira Seaman, Global English Academy, NY; Richard Seltzer, Glendale Community College, CA; Harlan Sexton, CUNY Queensborough Community College, NY; Kathy Sherak, San Francisco State University, CA; German Silva, Miami Dade College, FL; Ray Smith, Maryland English Institute, University of Maryland, MD; Shira Smith, NICE Program University of Hawaii, HI; Tara Smith, Felician College, NJ; Monica Snow, California State University, Fullerton, CA; Elaine Soffer, Nassau County Community College, NY; Andrea Spector, Santa Monica Community College, CA; Jacqueline Sport, LBWCC Luverne Center, AL; Karen Stanely, Central Piedmont Community College, NC; Susan Stern, Irvine Valley College, CA; Ayse Stromsdorfer, Soldan I.S.H.S., MO; Yilin Sun, South Seattle Community College, WA; Thomas Swietlik, Intrax International Institute, IL; Nicholas Taggert, University of Dayton, OH; Judith Tanka, UCLA Extension–American Language Center, CA; Amy Taylor, The University of Alabama Tuscaloosa, AL; Andrea Taylor, San Francisco State, CA; Priscilla Taylor, University of Southern California, CA; Ilene Teixeira, Fairfax County Public Schools, VA; Shirl H. Terrell, Collin College, TX; Marya Teutsch-Dwyer, St. Cloud State University, MN; Stephen Thergesen, ELS Language Centers, CO; Christine Tierney, Houston Community College, TX; Arlene Turini, North Moore High School, NC; Cara Tuzzolino, Nassau County Community College, NY; Suzanne Van Der Valk, Iowa State University, IA; Nathan D. Vasarhely, Ygnacio Valley High School, CA; Naomi S. Verratti, Howard Community College, MD; Hollyahna Vettori, Santa Rosa Junior College, CA; Julie Vorholt, Lewis & Clark College, OR; Danielle Wagner, FLS International Marymount College, CA; Lynn Walker, Coastline Community College, CA; Laura Walsh, City College of San Francisco, CA; Andrew J. Watson, The English Bakery; Donald Weasenforth, Collin College, TX; Juliane Widner, Sheepshead Bay High School, NY; Lynne Wilkins, Mills College, CA; Pamela Williams, Ventura College, CA; Jeff Wilson, Irvine Valley College, CA; James Wilson, Consomnes River College, CA; Katie Windahl, Cuyahoga Community College, OH; Dolores "Lorrie" Winter, California State University at Fullerton, CA; Jody Yamamoto, Kapi'olani Community College, HI; Ellen L. Yaniv, Boston University, MA; Norman Yoshida, Lewis & Clark College, OR; Joanna Zadra, American River College, CA; Florence Zysman, Santiago Canyon College, CA;

CANADA Patricia Birch, Brandon University, MB; Jolanta Caputa, College of New Caledonia, BC; Katherine Coburn, UBC's ELI, BC; Erin Harris-Macleod, St. Mary's University, NS; Tami Moffatt, English Language Institute, BC; Jim Papple, Brock University, ON; Robin Peace, Confederation College, BC;

ASIA Rabiatu Abubakar, Eton Language Centre, Malaysia; Wiwik Andreani, Bina Nusantara University, Indonesia; Frank Bailey, Baiko Gakuin University, Japan; Mike Baker, Kosei Junior High School, Japan; Leonard Barrow, Kanto Junior College, Japan; Herman Bartelen, Japan; Siren Betty, Fooyin University, Kaohsiung; Thomas E. Bieri, Nagoya College, Japan; Natalie Brezden, Global English House, Japan; MK Brooks, Mukogawa Women's University, Japan; Truong Ngoc Buu, The Youth Language School, Vietnam; Charles Cabell, Toyo University, Japan; Fred Carruth, Matsumoto University, Japan; Frances Causer, Seijo University, Japan; Jeffrey Chalk, SNU, South Korea; Deborah Chang, Wenzao Ursuline College of Languages, Kaohsiung; David Chatham, Ritsumeikan University, Japan; Andrew Chih Hong Chen, National Sun Yat-sen University, Kaohsiung; Christina Chen, Yu-Tsai Bilingual Elementary School, Taipei; Hui-chen Chen, Shi-Lin High School of Commerce, Taipei; Seungmoon Choe, K2M Language Institute, South Korea; Jason Jeffree Cole, Coto College, Japan; Le Minh Cong, Vungtau Tourism Vocational College, Vietnam; Todd Cooper, Toyama National College of Technology, Japan; Marie Cosgrove, Daito Bunka University, Japan; Randall Cotten, Gifu City Women's College, Japan; Tony Cripps, Ritsumeikan University, Japan; Andy Cubalit, CHS, Thailand; Daniel Cussen, Takushoku University, Japan; Le Dan, Ho Chi Minh City Electric Power College, Vietnam; Simon Daykin, Banghwa-dong Community Centre, South Korea; Aimee Denham, ILA, Vietnam; Bryan Dickson, David's English Center, Taipei; Nathan Ducker, Japan University, Japan; Ian Duncan, Simul International Corporate Training, Japan; Nguyen Thi Kieu Dung, Thang Long University, Vietnam; Truong Quang Dung, Tien Giang University, Vietnam; Nguyen Thi Thuy Duong, Vietnamese American Vocational Training College, Vietnam; Wong Tuck Ee, Raja Tun Azlan Science Secondary School, Malaysia; Emilia Effendy, International Islamic University Malaysia, Malaysia; Bettizza Escueta, KMUTT, Thailand; Robert Eva, Kaisei Girls High School, Japan; Jim George, Luna International Language School, Japan; Jurgen Germeys, Silk Road Language Center, South Korea; Wong Ai Gnoh, SMJK Chung Hwa Confucian, Malaysia; Sarah Go, Seoul Women's University, South Korea; Peter Goosselink, Hokkai High School, Japan; Robert Gorden, SNU, South Korea; Wendy M. Gough, St. Mary College/Nunoike Gaigo Senmon Gakko, Japan; Tim Grose, Sapporo Gakuin University, Japan; Pham Thu Ha, Le Van Tam Primary School, Vietnam; Ann-Marie Hadzima, Taipei; Troy Hammond, Tokyo Gakugei University International Secondary School, Japan; Robiatul 'Adawiah Binti Hamzah, SMK Putrajaya Precinct 8(1), Malaysia; Tran Thi Thuy Hang, Ho Chi Minh City Banking University, Vietnam; To Thi Hong Hanh, CEFALT, Vietnam; George Hays, Tokyo Kokusai Daigaku, Japan; Janis Hearn, Hongik University, South Korea; Chantel Hemmi, Jochi Daigaku, Japan; David Hindman, Sejong University, South Korea; Nahn Cam Hoa, Ho Chi Minh City University of Technology, Vietnam; Jana Holt, Korea University, South Korea; Jason Hollowell, Nihon University, Japan; F. N. (Zoe) Hsu, National Tainan University, Yong Kang; Kuei-ping Hsu, National Tsing Hua University, Hsinchu City; Wenhua Hsu, I-Shou University, Kaohsiung; Luu Nguyen Quoc Hung, Cantho University, Vietnam; Cecile Hwang, Changwon National University, South Korea; Ainol Haryati Ibrahim, Universiti Malaysia Pahang, Malaysia; Robert Jeens, Yonsei University, South Korea; Linda M. Joyce, Kyushu Sangyo University, Japan; Dr. Nisai Kaewsanchai, English Square Kanchanaburi, Thailand; Aniza Kamarulzaman, Sabah Science Secondary School, Malaysia; Ikuko Kashiwabara, Osaka Electro-Communication University, Japan; Gurmit Kaur, INTI College, Malaysia; Nick Keane, Japan; Ward Ketcheson, Aomori University, Japan; Nicholas Kemp, Kyushu International University, Japan; Montchatry Ketmuni, Rajamangala University of Technology, Thailand; Dinh Viet Khanh, Vietnam; Seonok Kim, Kangsu Jongro Language School, South Korea; Suyeon Kim, Anyang University, South Korea; Kelly P. Kimura, Soka University, Japan; Masakazu Kimura, Katoh Gakuen Gyoshu High School, Japan; Gregory King, Chubu Daigaku, Japan; Stan Kirk, Konan University, Japan; Donald Knight, Nan Hua/Fu Li Junior High Schools, Hsinchu; Kari J. Kostiainen, Nagoya City University, Japan; Pattri Kuanpulpol, Silpakorn University, Thailand; Ha Thi Lan, Thai Binh Teacher Training College, Vietnam; Eric Edwin Larson, Miyazaki Prefectural Nursing University, Japan; David Laurence, Chubu Daigaku, Japan; Richard S. Lavin, Prefectural University of Kumamoto, Japan; Shirley Leane, Chugoku Junior College, Japan; I-Hsiu Lee, Yunlin; Nari Lee, Park Jung PLS, South Korea; Tae Lee, Yonsei University, South Korea; Lys Yongsoon Lee, Reading Town Geumcheon, South Korea; Mallory Leece, Sun Moon University, South Korea; Dang Hong Lien, Tan Lam Upper Secondary School, Vietnam; Huang Li-Han, Rebecca Education Institute, Taipei; Sovannarith Lim, Royal University of Phnom Penh, Cambodia; Ginger Lin, National Kaohsiung Hospitality College, Kaohsiung; Noel Lineker, New Zealand/Japan; Tran Dang Khanh Linh, Nha Trang Teachers' Training College, Vietnam; Daphne Liu, Buliton English School, Taipei; S. F. Josephine Liu, Tien-Mu Elementary School, Taipei; Caroline Luo, Tunghai University, Taichung; Jeng-Jia Luo, Tunghai University, Taichung; Laura MacGregor, Gakushuin University, Japan; Amir Madani, Visuttharangsi School, Thailand; Elena Maeda, Sacred Heart Professional Training College, Japan; Vu Thi Thanh Mai, Hoang Gia Education Center, Vietnam; Kimura Masakazu, Kato Gakuen Gyoshu High School, Japan; Susumu Matsuhashi, Net Link English School, Japan; James McCrostie, Daito Bunka University, Japan; Joel McKee, Inha University, South Korea; Colin McKenzie, Wachirawit Primary School, Thailand; Terumi Miyazoe, Tokyo Denki Daigaku, Japan; William K. Moore, Hiroshima Kokusai Gakuin University, Japan; Kevin Mueller, Tokyo Kokusai Daigaku, Japan; Hudson Murrell, Baiko Gakuin University, Japan; Frances Namba, Senri International School of Kwansei Gakuin, Japan; Keiichi Narita, Niigata University, Japan; Kim Chung Nguyen, Ho Chi Minh University of

Industry, Vietnam; **Do Thi Thanh Nhan**, Hanoi University, Vietnam; **Dale Kazuo Nishi**, Aoyama English Conversation School, Japan; **Huynh Thi Ai Nguyen**, Vietnam; **Dongshin Oh**, YBM PLS, South Korea; **Keiko Okada**, Dokkyo Daigaku, Japan; **Louise Ohashi**, Shukutoku University, Japan; **Yongjun Park**, Sangji University, South Korea; **Donald Patnaude**, Ajarn Donald's English Language Services, Thailand; **Virginia Peng**, Ritsumeikan University, Japan; **Suangkanok Piboonthamnont**, Rajamangala University of Technology, Thailand; **Simon Pitcher**, Business English Teaching Services, Japan; **John C. Probert**, New Education Worldwide, Thailand; **Do Thi Hoa Quyen**, Ton Duc Thang University, Vietnam; **John P. Racine**, Dokkyo University, Japan; **Kevin Ramsden**, Kyoto University of Foreign Studies, Japan; **Luis Rappaport**, Cung Thieu Nha Ha Noi, Vietnam; **Lisa Reshad**, Konan Daigaku Hyogo, Japan; **Peter Riley**, Taisho University, Japan; **Thomas N. Robb**, Kyoto Sangyo University, Japan; **Rory Rosszell**, Meiji Daigaku, Japan; **Maria Feti Rosyani**, Universitas Kristen Indonesia, Indonesia; **Greg Rouault**, Konan University, Japan; **Chris Ruddenklau**, Kindai University, Japan; **Hans-Gustav Schwartz**, Thailand; **Mary-Jane Scott**, Soongsil University, South Korea; **Dara Sheahan**, Seoul National University, South Korea; **James Sherlock**, A.P.W. Angthong, Thailand; **Prof. Shieh**, Minghsin University of Science & Technology, Xinfeng; **Yuko Shimizu**, Ritsumeikan University, Japan; **Suzila Mohd Shukor**, Universiti Sains Malaysia, Malaysia; **Stephen E. Smith**, Mahidol University, Thailand; **Moon-young Son**, South Korea; **Seunghee Son**, Anyang University, South Korea; **Mi-young Song**, Kyungwon University, South Korea; **Lisa Sood**, VUS, BIS, Vietnam; **Jason Stewart**, Taejon International Language School, South Korea; **Brian A. Stokes**, Korea University, South Korea; **Mulder Su**, Shih-Chien University, Kaohsiung; **Yoomi Suh**, English Plus, South Korea; **Yun-Fang Sun**, Wenzao Ursuline College of Languages, Kaohsiung; **Richard Swingle**, Kansai Gaidai University, Japan; **Sanford Taborn**, Kinjo Gakuin Daigaku, Japan; **Mamoru Takahashi**, Akita Prefectural University, Japan; **Tran Hoang Tan**, School of International Training, Vietnam; **Takako Tanaka**, Doshisha University, Japan; **Jeffrey Taschner**, American University Alumni Language Center, Thailand; **Matthew Taylor**, Kinjo Gakuin Daigaku, Japan; **Michael Taylor**, International Pioneers School, Thailand; **Kampanart Thammaphati**, Wattana Wittaya Academy, Thailand; **Tran Duong The**, Sao Mai Language Center, Vietnam; **Tran Dinh Tho**, Duc Tri Secondary School, Vietnam; **Huynh Thi Anh Thu**, Nhatrang College of Culture Arts and Tourism, Vietnam; **Peter Timmins**, Peter's English School, Japan; **Fumie Togano**, Hosei Daini High School, Japan; **F. Sigmund Topor**, Keio University Language School, Japan; **Tu Trieu**, Rise VN, Vietnam; **Yen-Cheng Tseng**, Chang-Jung Christian University, Tainan; **Pei-Hsuan Tu**, National Cheng Kung University, Tainan City; **Hajime Uematsu**, Hirosaki University, Japan; **Rachel Um**, Mok-dong Oedae English School, South Korea; **David Underhill**, EEExpress, Japan; **Ben Underwood**, Kugenuma High School, Japan; **Siriluck Usaha**, Sripatum University, Thailand; **Tyas Budi Utami**, Indonesia; **Nguyen Thi Van**, Far East International School, Vietnam; **Stephan Van Eycken**, Kosei Gakuen Girls High School, Japan; **Zisa Velasquez**, Taihu International School/Semarang International School, China/Indonesia; **Jeffery Walter**, Sangji University, South Korea; **Bill White**, Kinki University, Japan; **Yohanes De Deo Widyastoko**, Xaverius Senior High School, Indonesia; **Dylan Williams**, SNU, South Korea; **Jisuk Woo**, Ichean University, South Korea; **Greg Chung-Hsien Wu**, Providence University, Taichung; **Xun Xiaoming**, BLCU, China; **Hui-Lien Yeh**, Chai Nan University of Pharmacy and Science, Tainan; **Sittiporn Yodnil**, Huachiew Chalermprakiet University, Thailand; **Shamshul Helmy Zambahari**, Universiti Teknologi Malaysia, Malaysia; **Ming-Yuli**, Chang Jung Christian University, Tainan; **Aimin Fadhlee bin Mahmud Zuhodi**, Kuala Terengganu Science School, Malaysia;

TURKEY **Shirley F. Akis**, American Culture Association/Fomara; **Gül Akkoç**, Boğaziçi University; **Seval Akmeşe**, Haliç University; **Ayşenur Akyol**, Ege University; **Ayşe Umut Aribaş**, Beykent University; **Gökhan Asan**, Kapadokya Vocational College; **Hakan Asan**, Kapadokya Vocational College; **Julia Asan**, Kapadokya Vocational College; **Azarvan Atac**, Piri Reis University; **Nur Babat**, Kapadokya Vocational College; **Feyza Balakbabalar**, Kadir Has University; **Gözde Balikçi**, Beykent University; **Deniz Balım**, Haliç University; **Asli Başdoğan**, Kadir Has University; **Ayla Bayram**, Kapadokya Vocational College; **Pinar Bilgiç**, Kadir Has University; **Kenan Bozkurt**, Kapadokya Vocational College; **Yonca Bozkurt**, Ege University; **Frank Carr**, Piri Reis; **Mengü Noyan Çengel**, Ege University; **Elif Doğan**, Ege University; **Natalia Donmez**, 29 Mayis Üniverste; **Nalan Emirsoy**, Kadir Has University; **Ayşe Engin**, Kadir Has University; **Ayhan Gedikbaş**, Ege University; **Gülşah Gençer**, Beykent University; **Seyit Ömer Gök**, Gediz University; **Tuğba Gök**, Gediz University; **İlkay Gökçe**, Ege University; **Zeynep Birinci Guler**, Maltepe University; **Neslihan Güler**, Kadir Has University; **Sircan Gümüş**, Kadir Has University; **Nesrin Gündoğu**, T.C. Piri Reis University; **Tanju Gurpinar**, Piri Reis University; **Selin Gurturk**, Piri Reis University; **Neslihan Gurutku**, Piri Reis University; **Roger Hewitt**, Maltepe University; **Nilüfer İbrahimoğlu**, Beykent University; **Nevin Kaftelen**, Kadir Has University; **Sultan Kalin**, Kapadokya Vocational College; **Sema Kaplan Karabina**, Anadolu University; **Eray Kara**, Giresun University; **Beylü Karayazgan**, Ege University; **Darren Kelso**, Piri Reis University; **Trudy Kittle**, Kapadokya Vocational College; **Şaziye Konaç**, Kadir Has University; **Güneş Korkmaz**, Kapadokya Vocational College; **Robert Ledbury**, Izmir University of Economics; **Ashley Lucas**, Maltepe University; **Bülent Nedium Uça**, Dogus University; **Murat Nurlu**, Ege University; **Mollie Owens**, Kadir Has University; **Oya Özağaç**, Boğaziçi University; **Funda Özcan**, Ege University; **İlkay Özdemir**, Ege University; **Ülkü Öztürk**, Gediz University; **Cassandra Puls**, Anadolu University; **Yelda Sarikaya**, Cappadocia Vocational College; **Müge Şekercioğlu**, Ege University; **Melis Senol**, Canakkale Onsekiz Mart University, The School of Foreign Languages; **Patricia Sümer**, Kadir Has University; **Rex Surface**, Beykent University; **Mustafa Torun**, Kapadokya Vocational College; **Tansel Üstünloğlu**, Ege University; **Fatih Yücel**, Beykent University; **Şule Yüksel**, Ege University;

THE MIDDLE EAST **Amina Saif Mohammed Al Hashamia**, Nizwa College of Applied Sciences, Oman; **Jennifer Baran**, Kuwait University, Kuwait; **Phillip Chappells**, GEMS Modern Academy, U.A.E.; **Sharon Ruth Devaneson**, Ibri College of Technology, Oman; **Hanaa El-Deeb**, Canadian International College, Egypt; **Yvonne Eaton**, Community College of Qatar, Qatar; **Brian Gay**, Sultan Qaboos University, Oman; **Gail Al Hafidh**, Sharjah Women's College (HCT), U.A.E.; **Jonathan Hastings**, American Language Center, Jordan; **Laurie Susan Hilu**, English Language Centre, University of Bahrain, Bahrain; **Abraham Irannezhad**, Mehre Aval, Iran; **Kevin Kempe**, CNA-Q, Qatar; **Jill Newby James**, University of Nizwa; **Mary Kay Klein**, American University of Sharjah, U.A.E.; **Sian Khoury**, Fujairah Women's College (HCT), U.A.E.; **Hussein Dehghan Manshadi**, Farhang Pajooh & Jaam-e-Jam Language School, Iran; **Jessica March**, American University of Sharjah, U.A.E.; **Neil McBeath**, Sultan Qaboos University, Oman; **Sandy McDonagh**, Abu Dhabi Men's College (HCT), U.A.E.; **Rob Miles**, Sharjah Women's College (HCT), U.A.E.; **Michael Kevin Neumann**, Al Ain Men's College (HCT), U.A.E.;

LATIN AMERICA **Aldana Aguirre**, Argentina; **Claudia Almeida**, Coordenação de Idiomas, Brazil; **Cláudia Arias**, Brazil; **Maria de los Angeles Barba**, FES Acatlan UNAM, Mexico; **Lilia Barrios**, Universidad Autónoma de Tamaulipas, Mexico; **Adán Beristain**, UAEM, Mexico; **Ricardo Böck**, Manoel Ribas, Brazil; **Edson Braga**, CNA, Brazil; **Marli Buttelli**, Mater et Magistra, Brazil; **Alessandra Campos**, Inova Centro de Linguas, Brazil; **Priscila Catta Preta Ribeiro**, Brazil; **Gustavo Cestari**, Access International School, Brazil; **Walter D'Alessandro**, Virginia Language Center, Brazil; **Lilian De Gennaro**, Argentina; **Mônica De Stefani**, Quality Centro de Idiomas, Brazil; **Julio Alejandro Flores**, BUAP, Mexico; **Mirian Freire**, CNA Vila Guilherme, Brazil; **Francisco Garcia**, Colegio Lestonnac de San Angel, Mexico; **Miriam Giovanardi**, Brazil; **Darlene Gonzalez Miy**, ITESM CCV, Mexico; **Maria Laura Grimaldi**, Argentina; **Luz Dary Guzmán**, IMPAHU, Colombia; **Carmen Koppe**, Brazil; **Monica Krutzler**, Brazil; **Marcus Murilo Lacerda**, Seven Idiomas, Brazil; **Nancy Lake**, CEL-LEP, Brazil; **Cris Lazzerini**, Brazil; **Sandra Luna**, Argentina; **Ricardo Luvisan**, Brazil; **Jorge Murilo Menezes**, ACBEU, Brazil; **Monica Navarro**, Instituto Cultural A. C., Mexico; **Joacyr Oliveira**, Faculdades Metropolitanas Unidas and Summit School for Teachers, Brazil; **Ayrton Cesar Oliveira de Araujo**, E&A English Classes, Brazil; **Ana Laura Oriente**, Seven Idiomas, Brazil; **Adelia Peña Clavel**, CELE UNAM, Mexico; **Beatriz Pereira**, Summit School, Brazil; **Miguel Perez**, Instituto Cultural, Mexico; **Cristiane Perone**, Associação Cultura Inglesa, Brazil; **Pamela Claudia Pogré**, Colegio Integral Caballito / Universidad de Flores, Argentina; **Dalva Prates**, Brazil; **Marianne Rampaso**, Iowa Idiomas, Brazil; **Daniela Rutolo**, Instituto Superior Cultural Británico, Argentina; **Maione Sampaio**, Maione Carrijo Consultoria em Inglês Ltda, Brazil; **Elaine Santesso**, TS Escola de Idiomas, Brazil; **Camila Francisco Santos**, UNS Idiomas, Brazil; **Lucia Silva**, Cooplem Idiomas, Brazil; **Maria Adela Sorzio**, Instituto Superior Santa Cecilia, Argentina; **Elcio Souza**, Unibero, Brazil; **Willie Thomas**, Rainbow Idiomas, Brazil; **Sandra Villegas**, Instituto Humberto de Paolis, Argentina; **John Whelan**, La Universidad Nacional Autonoma de Mexico, Mexico

# CONTENTS

**Q: What are you interested in?**

**Q: What makes a good school?**

**Q: How do you choose your food?**

**Q: What makes something fun?**

# UNIT 1

**VOCABULARY** ▶ collocations for hobbies and interests
**GRAMMAR** ▶ simple present of *be*; simple present of other verbs
**PRONUNCIATION** ▶ simple present third-person *-s /-es*
**SPEAKING** ▶ keeping a conversation going
**NOTE TAKING** ▶ writing important words

Social Psychology

**UNIT QUESTION**

# What are you interested in?

**A** Discuss these questions with your classmates.

1. What do you talk about with a new friend? Circle the topics. Add one topic.

| | |
|---|---|
| music | photos you see online |
| sports | family |
| movies | work |
| books | _____ |
| videos you see online | |

2. What activities do you like?

3. Look at the photo. What is this person doing? Are you interested in this activity?

**B** Listen to *The Q Classroom* online. Then answer these questions.

1. What did the students say? What are they interested in?

2. Do the students like the same things you like?

 **C** Go to the Online Discussion Board to discuss the Unit Question with your classmates.

# LISTENING

|  **LISTENING** | **Are You Interested in History?** |

You are going to listen to three conversations at a school. Think about what interests you.

## PREVIEW THE LISTENING

**A.** **VOCABULARY** Here are some words and phrases from the listening. Read the definitions. Then circle the correct word or phrase to complete each conversation.

> **belong to** (*verb*) 🔑 to be a member of a group
>
> **club** (*noun*) 🔑 a group of people—they meet and do things together
>
> **collect** (*verb*) 🔑 to get and keep many things because you like them
>
> **good at** (*phrase*) 🔑 can do something well
>
> **hobbies** (*noun*) activities—you do them for fun
>
> **interested in** (*phrase*) 🔑 enjoying an activity or a topic
>
> **team** (*noun*) 🔑 a group of people—they play a sport or a game together

🔑 Oxford 2000 keywords

1. A: Do you ( collect / (belong to) ) the math club?

   B: Yes, I do. We meet on Thursdays.

2. A: I like basketball, but I can't play it well.

   B: My roommate is very ( good at / team ) basketball. He can teach you.

3. A: Wow, you're a great soccer player! Are you on the soccer ( hobbies / team )?

   B: Thanks! Yes, I am.

4. A: What do you like to do?

   B: Oh, I have a lot of ( interested in / hobbies ). I play tennis, I go hiking, and I like poetry.

5. A: Is there a book ( team / club ) at this school?

   B: Yes, there is. We meet in the library every Wednesday night. It's fun!

hiking

6. A: You have a lot of postcards!

   B: I ( hobbies / collect ) them. I have more than 2,000 postcards from all over the world.

7. A: I like the museum. Are you ( belong to / interested in ) history?

   B: Yes. History is my favorite class.

**iQ** ONLINE **B.** Go online for more practice with the vocabulary.

**C.** Read the sentences. Circle *T* (true) or *F* (false). Then correct each false statement. Compare your answers with a partner.

1. T  F  I collect coins. _____

2. T  F  I belong to a book club. _____

3. T  F  I am interested in sports. _____

4. T  F  I am good at writing. _____

5. T  F  My hobbies are soccer and cooking. _____

**D.** PREVIEW  You are going to listen to three conversations at a school. Look at the pictures. Match each question with the correct picture.

1. ____         2. ____         3. ____

a. Can I sit here?

b. Is that a good book?

c. Is this Professor Kim's history class?

# WORK WITH THE LISTENING

**A.** Read the sentences. Then listen to all three conversations. Write *T* (true), *F* (false), or *N* (not enough information).

_____ 1. All the speakers are students.

_____ 2. All the speakers have hobbies.

_____ 3. All the speakers know each other well.

_____ 4. All the speakers live in the same city.

_____ 5. Some of the speakers play sports.

It's nice to meet you.

**B.** Listen again. What are the people interested in? Check (✓) the correct activities.

| 1. Lin | ☐ video games | ☐ hiking | ☐ books | ☐ history |
|---|---|---|---|---|
| Jane | ☐ video games | ☐ hiking | ☐ books | ☐ history |
| 2. David | ☐ books | ☐ cycling | ☐ poetry books | ☐ soccer |
| Alan | ☐ books | ☐ cycling | ☐ poetry books | ☐ soccer |
| 3. Sam | ☐ rugby | ☐ baseball | ☐ soccer | ☐ tennis |
| Maro | ☐ rugby | ☐ baseball | ☐ soccer | ☐ tennis |

**C.** Look at the chart in Activity B. Which people like the same activities?

1. _____ and _____ like history.

2. _____ , _____ , _____ ,

   and _____ like books.

3. _____ , _____ , _____ ,

   _____ , and _____ like outdoor activities.

**D.** Read the sentences. Then listen again. Circle the correct answers.

1. a. Lin goes hiking with her friends every

   ( Thursday / weekend / afternoon ).

   b. Jane belongs to the ( book / history / hiking ) club.

**2.** a. Alan's book club reads ( one / ten / twelve ) books a year.

   b. David is on the ( tennis / soccer / baseball ) team.

**3.** a. Sam's father is on a ( rugby / soccer / tennis ) team.

   b. Maro's favorite sport is ( tennis / soccer / baseball ).

**E.** Read these questions from the listening. What can you guess from the questions? Circle the correct answers.

**1.** "Excuse me. Can I sit here?"
   a. The speakers know each other.
   b. The speakers are both standing.
   c. One speaker is sitting. One is standing.

**2.** "Hi, Alan. Is that a good book?"
   a. The speakers know each other.
   b. Alan has a book.
   c. The speaker has a book.

**3.** "Hi, is this Professor Kim's history class?"
   a. The speakers know each other.
   b. The speakers are students.
   c. This is the first day of class.

 **F.** Go online to listen to *Ronaldinho, Brazilian Soccer Player* and check your comprehension.

## Building Vocabulary | Collocations for hobbies and interests

Some words usually go together. These are called **collocations**.

| Verb + preposition + noun | Verb + noun |
|---|---|
| **be good at** volleyball / math | **go** shopping / hiking |
| **be interested in** books / sports | **play** sports / tennis / games |
| **be on** a team | **read** books / magazines |
| **belong to** a book club | **ride** a bicycle / a bike |
| **get together with** friends | **take** lessons |
| **go to** a museum / the beach / a park | **watch** a DVD / television |
| **listen to** the radio | |
| **live in** Tokyo | |

**A.** Complete the collocations with words from the box above. Then listen to check your answers.

Alan lives _____ Toronto. He works at the after-school

1

program at the community center in his town. Children come to the

community center after school. Alan does many activities with them. It's

a good job for him because he is interested _____ a lot of

2

different things. He is good _____ sports. On sunny days,

3

Alan and the kids _____ bikes or _____

4                                                    5

hiking. Sometimes they go _____ the beach or the park.

6

On rainy days, Alan and the kids _____ DVDs, or they

7

_____ games like Scrabble and checkers. Sometimes they

8

_____ to a museum together. After work, Alan sometimes

9

gets _____ with friends, but he usually goes home to relax

10

and _____ a book.

11

**B.** Listen to the people talk about themselves. Write two sentences about each speaker. Use the words in parentheses.

1. **Saud** (reads) _____

   (is interested in) _____

2. **Khalid** (plays) _____

   (rides) _____

**C.** Write three sentences about you. Use collocations from the box on page 7.

iQ ONLINE **D.** Go online for more practice with collocations for hobbies and interests.

# SAY WHAT YOU THINK

**A.** Go around the class. Ask the questions from the chart. When someone answers *yes*, write down his or her name. Try to write a different name for each question.

*A: Do you ride a bicycle to class?*

*B: Yes, I do.*

I ride a bicycle to class.

| Question | Name |
|---|---|
| 1. Do you belong to a club? | |
| 2. Are you interested in books? | |
| 3. Do you play tennis? | |
| 4. Are you good at math? | |
| 5. Are you on a sports team? | |
| 6. Do you ride a bicycle to class? | |
| 7. Do you get together with friends on Thursdays? | |
| 8. Do you take any lessons? | |

 **for Success**

Use the word *too* to add information. It has the same meaning as *also*.

**B.** Share your answers with a group.

*A: Eric belongs to a soccer club.*

*B: Alex belongs to a soccer club, too.*

**iQ** ONLINE

**C.** Go online to watch a video about the Tate Modern Museum in London. Then check your comprehension.

**galleries** *(n.)* places where people can look at or buy art

**modern** *(adj.)* of the present time

**sculptures** *(n.)* art that is made from stone, wood, clay, or other material

VIDEO VOCABULARY

# SPEAKING

**UNIT OBJECTIVE** ▶▶▶ At the end of this unit, you are going to interview a classmate and introduce him or her to the class.

## Grammar | *Part 1* Simple present of *be*

 **Tip** for Success

Statements with *be* are followed by nouns (*a student*), adjectives (*tired*), or prepositional phrases (*from China*).

Use the verb *be* to identify and describe people and things.

| Statements | | | |
|---|---|---|---|
| subject | *be* | | |
| I | **am / 'm** | | a student. |
| You / We / They | **are / 're** | **(not)** | tired. |
| He / She / It | **is / 's** | | from China. |

- A contraction makes two words into one word. It has an apostrophe (').

  I am = I'm, You are = You're, They are = They're, He is = He's, She is = She's, It is = It's

- You usually use contractions in speaking.
- There are two negative contractions for *are not*.

  are not = 're not / aren't

  They're **not** happy.          They **aren't** tired.

- There are two negative contractions for *is not*.

  is not = 's not / isn't

  She's **not** American.          He **isn't** from England.

| Yes / No questions | | | Answers |
|---|---|---|---|
| *be* | subject | | |
| **Are** | you / we / they | in class? | Yes, I **am**. / No, we**'re** not. / Yes, they **are**. |
| **Is** | he / she | | No, she **isn't**. / Yes, he **is**. |

| Information questions | | | | Answers |
|---|---|---|---|---|
| *wh-* word | *be* | subject | | |
| **What** | **is** | she | interested in? | She**'s** interested in sports. |
| **Where** | **are** | they | from? | They**'re** from Morocco. |
| **How old** | **are** | you? | | I**'m** 22 years old. |

- You can give short answers or long answers:

  *A: How old are you?          B: 18. / I'm 18 years old.*

**A. Complete each conversation with the correct form of *be*.**

1. Mauro _is_ an artist. He isn't (not) from Colombia. He _____ from Peru.

2. Rika and Emiko _____ students. Rika _____ in my English class.

   Emiko _____ in my chemistry class. They _____ from Japan.

3. Feride _____ (not) American. She _____ Turkish.

4. I _____ (not) from England. I _____ from Ireland.

5. We _____ (not) interested in sports. We _____ interested in movies.

**B. Put the words in the correct order. Then ask and answer the questions with a partner.**

1. you / from / where / are _____ _Where are you from_ _____ ?

2. interested / history / you / in / are _____ ?

3. at / you / are / what / good _____ ?

4. years / 20 / old / you / are _____ ?

---

| Grammar | *Part 2* Simple present of other verbs |

Use the simple present with other verbs to describe habits, facts, and feelings.

| Affirmative statements | | |
|---|---|---|
| subject | verb | |
| I / You / We / They | **play** | soccer. |
| He / She | **plays** | tennis. |

| Negative statements | | |
|---|---|---|
| subject | *do / does + not* | verb |
| I / You / We / They | **do not / don't** | **play** baseball. |
| He / She | **does not / doesn't** | |

- Use *do not* with *I*, *we*, *you*, and *they*.
- Use *does not* with *he*, *she*, and *it*.

| Yes / No questions | | | | Answers |
|---|---|---|---|---|
| *do / does* | subject | verb | | |
| **Do** | you / we / they | **like** | tennis? | Yes, I **do**. / No, we **don't**. / Yes, they **do**. |
| **Does** | he / she | | | Yes, he **does**. / No, she **doesn't**. |

| Information questions | | | | Answers |
|---|---|---|---|---|
| *wh*- word | *do / does* | subject | | |
| **What** | **do** | you | play? | I play soccer. |
| **Where** | **does** | he | live? | He lives in Seoul. |
| **When** | **do** | they | study? | At 6:00. |

You can give short answers or long answers for these questions, too:
A: *Where do you live?*       B: *In Tokyo. / I live in Tokyo.*

**C.** Complete the conversations with the verbs from the box. Use the correct form. You will use some verbs more than once. Then practice with a partner.

| be | go | like | live | play | take |
|---|---|---|---|---|---|

1. **Sara:** Mary, what _____ you interested in?

   **Mary:** Well, I _____ hiking on the weekends. And

   on Fridays, I _____ French lessons.

2. **Emma:** _____ your brother interested in sports?

   **Mika:** Yes, he _____. He _____ soccer a lot.

3. **Anna:** _____ your parents from China?

   **Junko:** No, they _____. They _____ from

   Japan, but they _____ in the United States now.

4. **Joe:** _____ you good at Scrabble? I _____

   Scrabble a lot.

   **Rob:** No, I _____ good at Scrabble. But my brothers

   _____ Scrabble often.

**Scrabble™**

**D.** Put the words in the correct order. Then ask and answer the questions with a partner.

1. you / where / people / do / usually meet

   _____

2. know / do / on your street / people / you

   _____

3. your / do / what / you do / with / friends

   _____

4. you / go / friends / where / with / your / do

   _____

**E.** Go online for more practice with the simple present of *be* and other verbs.

**F.** Go online for the grammar expansion.

---

| Pronunciation | Simple present third-person *-s* / *-es* |
| --- | --- |

There are three ways to pronounce the final *-s* or *-es* of a simple present verb.

| / s / | | / z / | | / ɪz / | |
| --- | --- | --- | --- | --- | --- |
| ge**ts** | ma**kes** | liste**ns** | pla**ys** | wat**ches** | wa**shes** |

**A.** Listen to the sentences. Circle the sound that you hear at the end of the verb. Then practice the sentences with a partner.

**Critical Thinking** **Tip**

Activity A asks you to **identify** the sound you hear. This is one way to show you understand the lesson.

1. He goes shopping on Saturdays.      / s /    / z /    / ɪz /

2. Khalid works downtown.      / s /    / z /    / ɪz /

3. Sam plays video games in the evening.      / s /    / z /    / ɪz /

4. Sun-Hee sometimes watches TV after work.      / s /    / z /    / ɪz /

5. Mary gets together with friends on Sundays.      / s /    / z /    / ɪz /

6. Mika lives in Los Angeles.      / s /    / z /    / ɪz /

7. David washes his car on Saturdays.      / s /    / z /    / ɪz /

8. Miteb belongs to a golf club.      / s /    / z /    / ɪz /

**B.** Write five sentences about your friends. Use the verbs in the box.

| belongs | gets | goes | plays | takes | washes | watches |
|---------|------|------|-------|-------|--------|---------|

1. _____

2. _____

3. _____

4. _____

5. _____

**C.** Read your sentences from Activity B to a partner. For each of your partner's sentences, circle the sound you hear.

| **1.** / s / / z / / ɪz / | **3.** / s / / z / / ɪz / | **5.** / s / / z / / ɪz / |
|---|---|---|
| **2.** / s / / z / / ɪz / | **4.** / s / / z / / ɪz / | |

 **D.** Go online for more practice with simple present third-person verbs ending in *-s* and *-es*.

---

**Speaking Skill** | *Part 1* **Keeping a conversation going**

**Adding information**

Short answers to questions do not help conversations. Give extra information to keep your conversation going.

| Answer is too short. | Answer is good. |
|---|---|
| A: Rome is my favorite city. What's yours?<br>B: Shanghai. | A: Rome is my favorite city. What's yours?<br>B: Shanghai. It has amazing buildings and delicious food! |
| A: I like cooking. How about you?<br>B: I like cooking, too. | A: I like cooking. How about you?<br>B: I like cooking, too. I often cook with friends on the weekends. |

Tip for Success

Ask short questions like *How about you?* or *What's yours?* to get the other person's opinion or answer.

**A. Write answers to the questions. Add extra information. Then ask and answer the questions with a partner.**

1. A: What are your hobbies?

   B: _____

2. A: I like soccer. How about you?

   B: _____

3. A: What are you good at?

   B: _____

4. A: *Great Expectations* is my favorite book. What's yours?

   B: _____

5. A: Are you interested in history?

   B: _____

6. A: I'm interested in cooking. How about you?

   B: _____

## Speaking Skill  Part 2 Keeping a conversation going

### Taking time to think

Sometimes you can't answer a question right away. Use these special expressions before you answer. They tell people, "I am thinking."

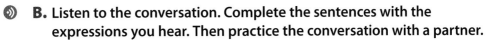

Hmm.    Let's see.    Let me see.    Let me think.    Uh.    Well.

**B. Listen to the conversation. Complete the sentences with the expressions you hear. Then practice the conversation with a partner.**

Tom: Carlos, what's your favorite sport?

Carlos: _____, it's soccer. But I also like basketball. What's yours?
       ¹

Tom: _____. It's probably volleyball. I play on the beach in
     ²
   the summer.

Carlos: Where's your favorite beach?

People surf at East Beach.

Tom: _____. Miami has a really good beach.
     ³

Carlos: _____, what's your favorite beach near here?
        ⁴

**Tom:** Ocean Beach is my favorite. It's beautiful! Do you know any beaches near here?

**Carlos:** _____. _____, I like East Beach. It has really
           5                    6

big waves. People surf there.

**C.** Work with a partner. Practice the questions and answers in Activity A on page 15 again. Use special expressions like *Hmm* and *Let me think.*

> **A:** *What are your hobbies?*
> **B:** *Let me think. I like games. I play Scrabble a lot.*

**iQ** ONLINE **D.** Go online for more practice with keeping a discussion going.

---

## Note-taking Skill | Writing important words

When you take notes, don't try to write down every word that you hear. Just write the important or meaningful words.

Read this sample from an interview.

| | |
|---|---|
| **Michael:** What's your name? | **Michael:** Do you have a job? |
| **Sung:** My name is Sung-bo Shin. You can call me Sung. | **Sung:** Yes, I do. I'm a construction worker. |
| **Michael:** Where are you from? | **Michael:** What are you interested in? |
| **Sung:** I'm from Seoul, South Korea. | **Sung:** I like to swim and run. I also like to paint. |

Look at the interviewer's notes. The interviewer only wrote the important words.

> *Sung-bo Shin (Sung)*
> *Seoul, South Korea*
> *construction worker*
> *swimming, running, painting*

---

## Unit Assignment | Interview and introduce a classmate

In this assignment, you are going to interview a classmate and introduce him or her to the class. Think about the Unit Question, "What are you interested in?" Use the listening, the unit video, and your work in this unit. Look at the Self-Assessment checklist on page 18.

# CONSIDER THE IDEAS

**A.** What do you say in an introduction? Check (✓) the information.

☐ a greeting          ☐ favorite book

☐ telephone number     ☐ hobbies and interests

☐ country           ☐ name

☐ job

**B.** Listen to this sample introduction. Then look at the list in Activity A. What information is in the introduction? Circle the ideas in Activity A.

> Good afternoon. This is my friend Ivan. Ivan is from Russia. He is a computer engineer. Ivan is interested in hiking in the mountains. He goes hiking once a month. Ivan is good at soccer. He belongs to a soccer club and plays every weekend. He gets together with his friends to play volleyball. Ivan reads a lot of books. His favorite book is *Treasure Island*.

# PREPARE AND SPEAK

**A.** FIND IDEAS Work with a partner. Follow these steps.

1. Add a question to the personal questionnaire below.

## Personal Questionnaire

1. What's your name?

2. Where are you from?

3. What's your favorite book?

4. What's your favorite food?

5. What are your hobbies and interests?

6. What are you good at?

7.

2. Use the questions to interview a partner. Write your partner's answers in the questionnaire on page 17. Write only the important words.

3. When you answer the questions, give extra information (not just short answers). Use special expressions like *Hmm* and *Let me think*.

**B.** Compare notes with your partner.

 **C.** Go online for more practice with taking notes on an interview.

**Tip** for Success

In your presentation, speak clearly so your classmates can hear you. Look at the audience.

**D.** **ORGANIZE IDEAS** Write three to five interesting sentences about your partner. Use the information from Activity A.

**E.** **SPEAK** Use your sentences to introduce your partner to the class. Include a greeting like "Good morning" and the introduction phrase "This is…." Look at the Self-Assessment checklist below before you begin.

 Go online for your alternate Unit Assignment.

## CHECK AND REFLECT

**A.** **CHECK** Think about the Unit Assignment as you complete the Self-Assessment checklist.

| SELF-ASSESSMENT | | |
|---|---|---|
| Yes | No | |
| ☐ | ☐ | My introduction was clear. |
| ☐ | ☐ | I used vocabulary from this unit. |
| ☐ | ☐ | I used the verb *be* and simple present statements correctly. |
| ☐ | ☐ | I included interesting information about my partner. |
| ☐ | ☐ | I took notes using only important words. |

 **B.** **REFLECT** Go to the Online Discussion Board to discuss these questions.

1. What is something new you learned in this unit?

2. Think about the Unit Question—What are you interested in? Is your answer different now than when you started this unit? If yes, how is it different? Why?

# TRACK YOUR SUCCESS

**Circle the words and phrases you have learned in this unit.**

**Nouns**
club 🔑
hobby
team 🔑 AWL

**Verbs**
belong to 🔑
collect 🔑

**Phrases**
good at 🔑
interested in 🔑

**Collocations**
be good at volleyball /
   math
be interested in books /
   sports
be on a team
belong to a book club
get together with friends
go to a museum /
   the beach / a park
listen to the radio

live in Tokyo
go shopping / hiking
play sports / tennis /
   games
read books / magazines
ride a bicycle / a bike
take lessons
watch a DVD / television

🔑 Oxford 2000 keywords
AWL Academic Word List

**Check (✓) the skills you learned. If you need more work on a skill, refer to the page(s) in parentheses.**

| | |
|---|---|
| **VOCABULARY** ■ | I can understand collocations for hobbies and interests. (p. 7) |
| **GRAMMAR** ■ | I can use the simple present of *be* and other verbs. (pp. 10–12) |
| **PRONUNCIATION** ■ | I can pronounce simple present third-person *-s* / *-es*. (p. 13) |
| **SPEAKING** ■ | I can keep a conversation going. (pp. 14–15) |
| **NOTE TAKING** ■ | I can write important words when taking notes. (p. 16) |
| **UNIT OBJECTIVE** ▶▶▶ ■ | I can use information and ideas to interview a classmate and introduce him or her to the class. |

UNIT **2**

Education

| LISTENING | ▶ | listening for examples |
| NOTE TAKING | ▶ | taking notes on examples |
| VOCABULARY | ▶ | using the dictionary: antonyms |
| GRAMMAR | ▶ | adjectives; adverbs + adjectives |
| PRONUNCIATION | ▶ | sentence stress |
| SPEAKING | ▶ | giving opinions |

**UNIT QUESTION**

# What makes a good school?

**A** Discuss these questions with your classmates.

1. How many students go to your school?

2. How many students are in your class?

3. Does your school have any clubs? Does your school have any sports teams?

4. Look at the photo. Does your school have classes like this one? What kinds of classes does your school have?

UNIT
OBJECTIVE ▶▶▶ Listen to a tour. Use information and ideas to give a
presentation about planning a perfect school.

🔊 **B** Listen to *The Q Classroom* online. Then
answer these questions.

1. What did the students say? What do each of
the four students like in a school?

2. Who do you agree with? Which ideas are less
important to you?

iQ ONLINE **C** Go online to watch a video about schools in Japan.
Then check your comprehension.

**bow** *(v.)* bend your head or
body forward

**quality** *(n.)* how good or bad
something is

**retire** *(v.)* to stop working because
you are a certain age

VIDEO VOCABULARY

iQ ONLINE **D** Go to the Online Discussion Board
to discuss the Unit Question
with your classmates.

21

**LISTENING** | ## Let's Take a Tour

 **UNIT OBJECTIVE** ▶▶▶ **You are going to listen to someone give a campus tour to university students. Think about what makes a good school.**

## PREVIEW THE LISTENING

**A.** **VOCABULARY** **Here are some words and phrases from the listening. Read the sentences. Which explanation is correct? Circle *a* or *b*.**

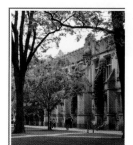

a school campus

1. My university has a big <u>campus</u>. It has more than 100 buildings.
   a. A campus is all the buildings and areas at a school.
   b. A campus is the students and the teachers at a school.

2. Matt can't go on the <u>Internet</u> in his room. He goes to a café to check his email.
   a. Matt can go online in his room.
   b. Matt can't go online in his room.

3. Mary has a great math <u>professor</u>. His classes are always interesting.
   a. A professor is a university student.
   b. A professor is a university teacher.

4. John gets good grades, so he is in <u>special</u> classes. His classes are difficult.
   a. John's classes are different or unusual.
   b. John's classes are normal or regular.

> **Tip for Success**
>
> The word *school* can refer to any educational institute. The words *college* and *university* often have the same meaning.

5. James is <u>active</u>. He plays soccer and basketball. He also belongs to the Spanish club.
   a. James does a lot of things.
   b. James has a lot of friends.

6. Writing is an important <u>skill</u>. Emma writes every day. She wants to be a good writer.
   a. Playing tennis is also a skill.
   b. Watching television is also a skill.

7. David is from France. For David, Korean is a <u>foreign language</u>.
   a. French is also a foreign language for David.
   b. Spanish is also a foreign language for David.

8. A <u>community</u> is a group of people. They live or work in the same area.
   a.  A bus stop is a kind of community.
   b.  A town is a kind of community.

**B.** Complete the sentences with words from Activity A.

1.  At my school, all of the students study a _____. I'm in a Japanese class.

2.  Rob's university has a really small _____. You can walk across it in ten minutes.

3.  A class is a kind of _____. The teachers and students work together.

4.  I have to talk to my biology _____. I have a question about the test.

5.  My brother is very _____. He takes five classes, plays soccer, and is a volunteer.

6.  Reading is an important _____. Good students read well.

 **C.** Go online for more practice with the vocabulary.

**D.** **PREVIEW** You are going to listen to a student give a tour of Watson University. Look at the map. Then match the names of the places with the definitions.

Watson University

1.  library ____          a.  Students live here.

2.  dormitory ____        b.  Students play games here.

3.  sports field ____     c.  There are a lot of books here.

4.  dining hall ____      d.  Students eat here.

**E.** Does your school have the four places in Activity D on page 23? What are some other places at your school?

## WORK WITH THE LISTENING

**A.** Read the sentences. Listen to the tour. Write *T* (true) or *F* (false) for each statement. Then correct each false statement to make it true.

_____ 1. There is free Internet access in the dining hall.

_____

_____ 2. About half of the students live on campus.

_____

_____ 3. The school has about 2,000 students.

_____

_____ 4. The professors want students to sit and listen quietly.

_____

_____ 5. The university is in a small town.

_____

_____ 6. Students spend a lot of time in town.

_____

**B.** Read the questions. Then circle the correct answers.

1. Where are the students?
   a. at Watson University
   b. in Watkins City
   c. in Washington

2. What are the students doing?
   a. talking with a professor
   b. taking a tour of a campus
   c. studying with friends

3. What is special about this university?
   a. It's very large, so there are many interesting classes.
   b. Students come from many different countries.
   c. It's small, so you can talk to your professors every day.

**iQ ONLINE** **C.** Go online to listen to *Student Exchange Programs* and check your comprehension.

## Listening Skill | Listening for examples

People give examples with **like**. *Like* comes in the middle of a sentence.

☐ I study in different places, **like** the library or my dormitory.

People also give examples with **for example**. *For example* can come at the beginning of a sentence.

☐ Watson University has many interesting classes. **For example**, I have classes in French and history.

**A.** Listen again to the tour of Watson University. Circle the correct answers.

1. What teams does Watson University have?
   a. lacrosse and soccer
   b. football and lacrosse
   c. football and tennis
   d. soccer and tennis

2. Why are small classes important?
   a. Small classes are very quiet.
   b. Small classes are busy.
   c. Professors know the students well.
   d. Professors talk a lot.

3. At Watson University, students are active. What example does Sarah give?
   a. They make special lessons.
   b. They give presentations.
   c. They have discussion groups.
   d. They work alone.

4. Students learn important skills. What example does Sarah give?
   a. study skills
   b. listening skills
   c. speaking skills
   d. writing skills

5. How can students help the community in the town of Watson?
   a. go to dinner
   b. become volunteers
   c. go to the library
   d. teach foreign languages

lacrosse

**iQ ONLINE** **B.** Go online for more practice with listening for examples.

## Note-taking Skill | Taking notes on examples

It is good to write down examples. Writing them in a chart helps you remember them. Listen to two students talk about college. Then look at the chart below. It shows examples of things the students talk about.

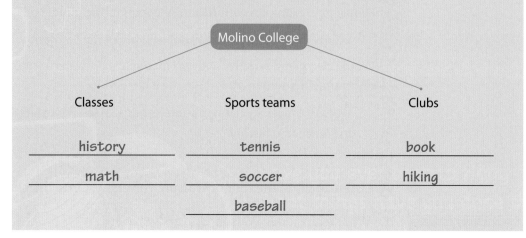

Molino College

| Classes | Sports teams | Clubs |
|---------|--------------|-------|
| history | tennis | book |
| math | soccer | hiking |
| | baseball | |

**A.** Listen again to the tour of Watson University. Work with a partner to complete the chart with examples.

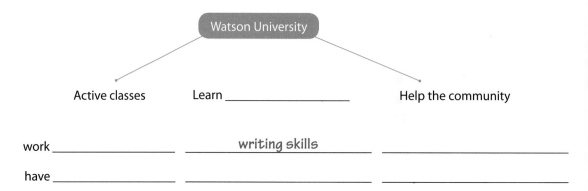

Watson University

| Active classes | Learn _____ | Help the community |
|----------------|---------------------|--------------------|
| work _____ | writing skills | _____ |
| have _____ | _____ | _____ |

**iQ ONLINE** **B.** Go online for more practice with taking notes on examples.

**Antonyms** are words with opposite meanings. For example, *good* and *bad* are antonyms. Most forms of words—nouns, verbs, adjectives, adverbs, and prepositions—can have antonyms.

The dictionary often gives antonyms in the definition of a word. In the example below, notice the antonyms of *hard*.

---

**hard**[1] 🔑 /hɑrd/ *adjective* (hard·er, hard·est)
**1** not soft: *These apples are very hard.* ◆ *I couldn't sleep because the bed was too hard.* ➲ ANTONYM **soft**
**2** difficult to do or understand: *The exam was very hard.* ◆ *hard work* ➲ ANTONYM **easy**
**3** full of problems: *He's had **a hard life**.* ➲ ANTONYM **easy**
**4** not kind or gentle: *She is very **hard on** her children.* ➲ ANTONYM **soft**

---

All dictionary entries are from the *Oxford Basic American Dictionary for learners of English* © Oxford University Press 2011.

**A.** Write an antonym for each word. Use the words in the box. Use your dictionary to help you.

| | | | |
|---|---|---|---|
| above | cheap | easy | strength |
| badly | complicated | negative | succeed |

1. hard _____

2. fail _____

3. below _____

4. weakness _____

5. positive _____

6. simple _____

7. expensive _____

8. well _____

**We have many discussions.**

**B.** Read the sentences. Circle the correct words.

1. Sun-Hee doesn't like her school. The classrooms are always ( clean / dirty ).

2. In my history class, we have many discussions and presentations. I like it a lot. It's very ( interesting / boring ).

3. One ( strength / weakness ) of my school is the library. It's very small, and it doesn't have a lot of books.

4. The school is in a ( safe / dangerous ) part of town. Don't go out late at night.

5. My school costs a lot of money. It's very ( cheap / expensive ).

6. In a good school, all of the students ( fail / succeed ).

7. Sarah lives ( on / off ) campus. Her dormitory is near the library.

8. My math class is really ( easy / hard ). I know all of the answers.

**C. Choose three adjectives. Write a sentence for each adjective and its antonym.**

My chemistry class is <u>hard</u>.     Math is <u>easy</u> for me.

 **D.** Go online for more practice with using the dictionary.

 **SAY WHAT YOU THINK**

**A.** Give your opinion of the following statements. Circle *Yes* or *No*.

### What makes a good school?

1. Yes   No   It's important to learn a foreign language in school.
2. Yes   No   It's important to have good friends at school.
3. Yes   No   Every school needs a lot of clubs and teams.
4. Yes   No   A good school has computers for students to use.
5. Yes   No   Every campus needs a library and a sports field.
6. Yes   No   Good schools have small classes.
7. Yes   No   A good school has a large campus.
8. Yes   No   A good school is a community.
9. Yes   No   A good school has new buildings.
10. Yes   No   Good schools are always in big cities.
11. Yes   No   In good schools, students can talk to teachers outside of class.
12. Yes   No   In a good class, students can ask the teacher questions.

**Critical Thinking Tip**

In Activity B, you **discuss** your answers. This helps you understand the information better.

**B. Discuss your answers with a partner. Tell your partner your reasons for your opinions.**

# SPEAKING

▶▶▶ At the end of this unit, you are going to give a group presentation about a perfect school.

---

| Grammar | Adjectives; Adverbs + adjectives |

### Adjectives

1. Adjectives describe nouns (people, places, things, or ideas).

   • An adjective can come after the verbs *be* or *have*. It describes the subject.

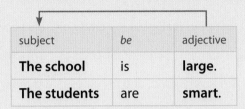

| subject | *be* | adjective |
|---|---|---|
| **The school** | is | **large.** |
| **The students** | are | **smart.** |

   • An adjective can come before a noun. It describes the noun.

| | adjective | noun |
|---|---|---|
| It's a | **safe** | **school.** |
| I have | **good** | **classes.** |

2. There are no singular or plural adjectives.

   ✓ Correct: They are **interesting classes**.
   ✗ Incorrect: They are interestings classes.

3. Do not use an article (*the*, *a*, or *an*) before an adjective with no noun.

   ✓ Correct: The class is **interesting**.
   ✗ Incorrect: The class is an interesting.

### Adverbs + adjectives

1. Adverbs make adjectives stronger.

   It's a **pretty** interesting class.       It's a **very** safe school.
   That school is **really** safe!       This classroom is **extremely** noisy!

   • Use *pretty* in speaking and informal writing. Don't use it in papers for your classes.

**2.** You can use *pretty*, *really*, *very*, and *extremely* before:

  an adjective alone: That school is **really excellent**.
  an adjective + a noun: It's a **very active class**.

**A.** Read the paragraph. Find the ten adjective and adverb errors and correct them.

> new university
> Well, I am now at my ~~university new~~. It's in a large very city. It's pretty
> different from our small town. It's an extremely noisy, but I love it. There are
> excellents museums and parks. I live in an apartment expensive in the city.
> The building is beautiful really, but it's pretty old. My school is great, but my
> classes are big extremely. Some of my classes have 200 people in them! But
> my professors are a very good, and my classes are really interesting. We have a
> science laboratory great. I study biology there. Also, the people here are friendly
> very, but I miss my old friends.

**B.** Complete the conversation with adjectives or adverbs + adjectives.
Use your own ideas. Then practice with a partner.

**A:** Do you like this school?

**B:** Yes, I do. I think that it's a _____ _____

school. What do you think?

**A:** I like it, too. The teachers are _____, and the classes are

_____.

**B:** What do you think of the library?

**A:** I think that it's _____ _____. What do you

think of the campus?

**B:** I think that it's _____ _____.

**C.** Go online for more practice with adjectives and adverbs + adjectives.

**D.** Go online for the grammar extension.

When you speak, you **stress** certain **important words**. This means you say them a little more loudly.

Important words—like nouns, adjectives, and adverbs—give the information in the sentences.

You do not usually stress words like pronouns, prepositions, *a / an / the*, the verb *be*, or the verb *do*.

There are **two sports fields**.
The **museum** is **not interesting**.
We **go** to **school** in a **really dangerous neighborhood**.
Do you **have** a **class today**?

**A.** Underline the stressed words. Listen and check your answers. Then practice the sentences with a partner.

1. Does the school have a fencing team?

2. I have two classes in the morning.

3. We want a safe and clean school.

4. The college is in a dangerous city.

5. The coffee shops have free Internet access.

6. What is a good school?

7. Our sports field is pretty big.

8. My school is really great!

fencing

**B.** Write five sentences about your school. Use adjectives and the adverbs *pretty*, *really*, *very*, and *extremely*.

**C.** Work with a partner. Read each other's sentences. Underline the stressed words. Then practice the sentences.

The <u>campus</u> is <u>extremely</u> <u>large</u>.

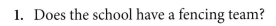 **D.** Go online for more practice with sentence stress.

Use the phrases *I think that…* and *In my opinion, …* to give an opinion.

**I think that** students need computers.
**In my opinion**, small classes are important.

You can answer opinions with *I agree* or *I disagree* followed by your opinion.

A: **I think that** our school is great.
B: **I agree.** I think that the classes are interesting.
C: **I disagree.** In my opinion, the classes are too big.

**A.** Listen and complete the conversations. Use expressions from the box above. Compare answers with a partner.

**Tip for Success**

When you write
*In my opinion*, use
a comma after it.
Don't use a comma
after *I think that*.

1. A: _____ a good school gives a lot of tests.

   Then students study every day.

   B: _____. Class discussions make students study.

2. A: _____ sports are really important. Students

   need healthy bodies.

   B: _____. Exercise is very important.

3. A: _____ the food in our dining hall isn't very

   good. I don't like it!

   B: _____. _____ it

   tastes terrible. I usually cook my own food.

4. A: Our school isn't in a good neighborhood. _____

   it's very dangerous. I hear police sirens all the time.

   B: _____. You hear sirens because the police

   station is on the same street! _____ the

   school is very safe.

**B.** Write answers to the questions. Start your answers with *I think that* or *In my opinion*. Then ask and answer the questions with a partner.

1. What is the perfect number of students in a foreign language class?

_____

2. In your opinion, what makes a class interesting? Give two ideas.

_____

3. Do you think it's better to work alone or with a group? Why?

_____

 **C.** Go online for more practice with giving your opinion.

---

**Unit Assignment**  Plan a perfect school

 In this assignment, you are going to plan a perfect school. This can be a high school, university, or other kind of school. Then you are going to present your plan to the class. Think about the Unit Question, "What makes a good school?" Use the listening, the unit video, and your work in this unit. Look at the Self-Assessment checklist on page 34.

## CONSIDER THE IDEAS

Listen to a group present their ideas for a perfect school. Check (✓) the ideas that they give. Then compare answers with a partner.

☐ 1. The perfect school is large.
☐ 2. The classes are very small.
☐ 3. The school has a lot of clubs, like a book club and a soccer club.
☐ 4. There is a big gym.
☐ 5. Students get free computers.
☐ 6. The school is in a big city.
☐ 7. Apartments in town are cheap and beautiful.
☐ 8. Food on campus is cheap.

## PREPARE AND SPEAK

 **for Success**

Examples can make your opinion strong and clear: *I think that a good school needs a sports field, **like a soccer field. Students need exercise. It makes them healthy.***

**A. FIND IDEAS** Work with a group. Write answers for these questions. Use *I think that* and *In my opinion*, to share your ideas.

1. Is your perfect school big or small? How many students are in a class?

2. What does the school have? For example, does it have a swimming pool? Does it have computers?

3. Is your school in a big city or a small town? What can students do there?

4. What is special about your school? How is it different from other schools?

**B.** `ORGANIZE IDEAS` **Work with your group. Prepare your presentation.**

1. Each group member chooses at least one question from Activity A on page 33.

2. Write your part of the presentation. Include at least one example or detail for your idea.

3. First speaker: Use these sentences as your introduction.

   *Good (morning / afternoon / evening). Today we are presenting our plan for a perfect school.*

4. Last speaker: Use these sentences as your conclusion.

   *That's the end of our presentation. Thank you for listening. Do you have any questions?*

**C.** `SPEAK` **Present your ideas to your class. Look at the Self-Assessment checklist below before you begin.**

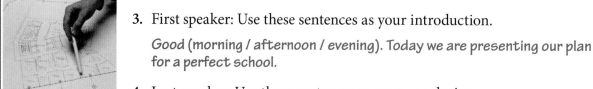 **Go online for your alternate Unit Assignment.**

## CHECK AND REFLECT

**A.** `CHECK` **Think about the Unit Assignment as you complete the Self-Assessment checklist.**

| SELF-ASSESSMENT | | |
|:---:|:---:|:---|
| **Yes** | **No** | |
| ☐ | ☐ | I gave my opinion clearly. |
| ☐ | ☐ | I used vocabulary from this unit. |
| ☐ | ☐ | I used adjectives and adverbs + adjectives correctly. |
| ☐ | ☐ | I stressed words in sentences correctly. |

 **B.** `REFLECT` **Go to the Online Discussion Board to discuss these questions.**

1. What is something new you learned in this unit?

2. Think about the Unit Question—What makes a good school? Is your answer different now than when you started this unit? If yes, how is it different? Why?

# TRACK YOUR SUCCESS

**Circle the words you have learned in this unit.**

**Nouns**
campus
community 🔑 AWL
foreign language 🔑
Internet 🔑
professor
skill 🔑
strength 🔑
weakness 🔑

**Verbs**
fail 🔑
succeed 🔑

**Adjectives**
active 🔑
boring 🔑
cheap 🔑
clean 🔑
complicated 🔑
dangerous 🔑
dirty 🔑
easy 🔑
expensive 🔑
hard 🔑
interesting 🔑
negative 🔑 AWL
positive 🔑 AWL
safe 🔑

simple 🔑
special 🔑

**Adverbs**
badly 🔑
extremely 🔑
pretty 🔑
really 🔑
very 🔑
well 🔑

**Prepositions**
above 🔑
below 🔑
off 🔑
on 🔑

🔑 Oxford 2000 keywords
AWL Academic Word List

**Check (✓) the skills you learned. If you need more work on a skill, refer to the page(s) in parentheses.**

| | |
|---|---|
| **LISTENING** ☐ | I can identify examples. (p. 25) |
| **NOTE TAKING** ☐ | I can take notes on examples. (p. 26) |
| **VOCABULARY** ☐ | I can use the dictionary to understand antonyms. (p. 27) |
| **GRAMMAR** ☐ | I can use adjectives and adverbs + adjectives. (p. 29) |
| **PRONUNCIATION** ☐ | I can stress important words. (p. 31) |
| **SPEAKING** ☐ | I can give my opinion. (p. 32) |
| **UNIT OBJECTIVE** ▶▶▶ ☐ | I can use information and ideas to present a plan about a perfect school. |

| VOCABULARY | ▷ | prefixes and suffixes |
| PRONUNCIATION | ▷ | stressed syllables |
| LISTENING | ▷ | listening for reasons |
| GRAMMAR | ▷ | verbs + gerunds or infinitives |
| NOTE TAKING | ▷ | taking notes on an interview |
| SPEAKING | ▷ | review: giving opinions |

UNIT QUESTION

# How do you choose your food?

**A** Discuss these questions with your classmates.

1. Circle the adjectives that describe food. Compare with a partner.

| active | spicy | dangerous | sour |
| delicious | close | healthy | difficult |
| fresh | important | salty | sweet |

2. Describe your favorite food. Where do you shop for food?

3. Look at the photos. Where do these people get their food?

**⏺ B Listen to *The Q Classroom* online. Then answer these questions.**

1. What did the students say about the foods they like?

2. Which student likes spicy food? Who doesn't eat sugar?

3. What foods do you like? For example, do you like spicy food? Why or why not?

 **C Go online to watch the video about a family's food choices. Then check your comprehension.**

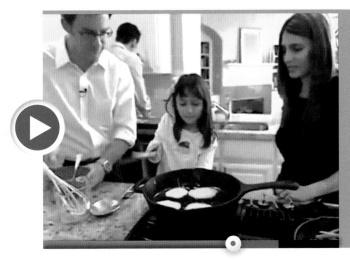

VIDEO VOCABULARY

**grind** *(v.)* to break something into very small pieces or a powder

**inviting** *(v.)* asking someone to come to an event or a place

**locavore** *(n.)* a person who eats only food grown or made near home

 **D Go to the Online Discussion Board to discuss the Unit Question with your classmates.**

## LISTENING | Lifestyles and Food Choices

**UNIT OBJECTIVE** ▶▶▶ You are going to listen to a reporter interview people in a supermarket. Think about how you choose your food.

### PREVIEW THE LISTENING

**A.** **VOCABULARY** Here are some words from the listening. Read the definitions. Then complete the sentences below.

> **avoid** (*verb*) 🔑 to try not to do something
> **flavor** (*noun*) 🔑 the taste of food, like salty or sweet
> **ingredient** (*noun*) one of the things that are used to make food
> **nutritious** (*adjective*) good for you
> **organic** (*adjective*) natural; organic food has only natural ingredients
> **social** (*adjective*) 🔑 likes to be with other people
> **vegetarian** (*noun*) a person who does not eat meat

🔑 Oxford 2000 keywords

ingredients

1. I put tomato sauce, garlic, cheese, and onions in my pasta. It has a lot of _____.

2. Fruits are _____. For example, oranges have vitamin C.

3. Rob is a _____ person. He spends a lot of time with his friends.

4. Amanda and Matt _____ food with a lot of fat. For example, they don't eat French fries or cheeseburgers.

5. Lemons are sour, but oranges have a sweet _____.

6. Sam doesn't eat chicken or beef. He's a _____.

7. John buys his food at a health-food store. He eats only _____ food.

**B.** Answer the questions. Then compare with a partner.

1. What is an example of a food with a strong flavor? _____

2. Are you a vegetarian or do you eat meat? _____

3. How often do you eat organic food? _____

4. Do you avoid food with artificial ingredients? _____

   Why or why not? _____

5. Name three foods that are very nutritious. _____

   _____

**iQ** ONLINE  **C.** Go online for more practice with the vocabulary.

**D.** PREVIEW  You are going to listen to a reporter interview four people. She asks, "How do you choose your food?" She learns about the way the people live.

What questions do you think about when you choose your food?
Check (✓) the questions.

1. ☐ Is it good for me?

2. ☐ Does it have a lot of sugar in it?

3. ☐ Does it have a lot of fat in it?

4. ☐ Is it organic?

5. ☐ Does it taste good?

6. ☐ How much does it cost?

7. ☐ Is it easy to get or use?

8. ☐ Does it have meat in it?

# WORK WITH THE LISTENING

**A.** Listen to the four conversations. Write *T* (true) or *F* (false) for each sentence. Correct the false statements.

_____ 1.  Carlos eats all foods.

_____

_____ 2.  Mika likes to make dinner for her friends.

_____

_____ 3.  Matt eats a lot of fresh fruits and vegetables.

_____

_____ 4.  Matt is 61 years old.

_____

_____ 5.  Sarah likes to cook at home.

_____

_____ 6.  Sarah is a busy student.

_____

**B.** Look at the chart. Then listen again. Check (✓) the correct information about each person.

I'm very careful about food.

| Carlos | Mika | Matt | Sarah | |
|--------|------|------|-------|---|
| ☑ | ☐ | ☐ | ☐ | a. is a vegetarian. |
| ☐ | ☐ | ☐ | ☐ | b. eats only organic food. |
| ☐ | ☐ | ☐ | ☐ | c. likes to taste new flavors. |
| ☐ | ☐ | ☐ | ☐ | d. thinks meat is bad for you. |
| ☐ | ☐ | ☐ | ☐ | e. doesn't have a kitchen. |
| ☐ | ☐ | ☐ | ☐ | f. avoids food with a lot of fat and salt. |
| ☐ | ☐ | ☐ | ☐ | g. chooses food that is easy to get or use. |
| ☐ | ☐ | ☐ | ☐ | h. eats nutritious food, like fish. |
| ☐ | ☐ | ☐ | ☐ | i. is 71 years old. |

**C.** **Write answers to the questions.**

1. Which two speakers are the most similar? How?

   _____

2. Which two speakers are the most different? How?

   _____

3. Which speaker is most similar to you? How?

   _____

4. Which speaker is most different from you? How?

   _____

5. Think about the unit video and the listening. How are Maggie Arroyos
   and Mika similar?

   _____

**D.** **Complete the Venn diagram. Show how you and the speaker from
question 3 in Activity C are similar and different.**

Speaker: _____          You

**E.** **Who is more careful about food choices? Number the people from 1
(most careful) to 4 (least careful). Talk with a partner. Compare and
explain your answers.**

____ Carlos          ____ Matt

____ Mika          ____ Sarah

**F.** Go online to listen to *Breakfast in Different Countries* and check your comprehension.

A **prefix** comes at the beginning of a word. It changes the meaning of the word. A **suffix** comes at the end of a word. It often changes the part of speech. Learners' dictionaries usually give definitions for prefixes and suffixes. Other dictionaries often list them at the back.

The prefixes *non-* and *un-* mean "not." The suffix *-free* means "without," and it changes a noun (*sugar*) into an adjective (*sugar-free*). Look at the definitions.

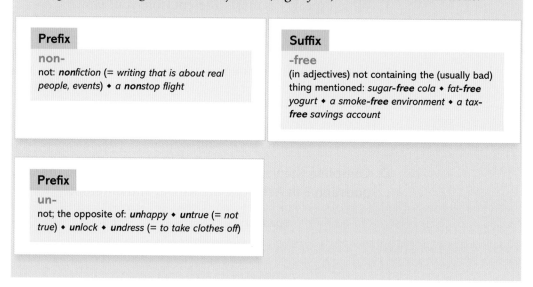

**Prefix**

**non-**
not: ***non**fiction* (= writing that is about real people, events) ◆ *a **non**stop flight*

**Suffix**

**-free**
(in adjectives) not containing the (usually bad) thing mentioned: *sugar-**free** cola* ◆ *fat-**free** yogurt* ◆ *a smoke-**free** environment* ◆ *a tax-**free** savings account*

**Prefix**

**un-**
not; the opposite of: ***un**happy* ◆ ***un**true* (= not true) ◆ ***un**lock* ◆ ***un**dress* (= to take clothes off)

All dictionary entries are from the *Oxford Basic American Dictionary for learners of English* © Oxford University Press 2011.

**A.** Read the sentences. Complete each sentence with a word in the box.

| | | | |
|---|---|---|---|
| nondairy | salt-free | unfriendly | unsafe |
| nonfat | sugar-free | unhealthy | unusual |

☐ 1. I worry about foods with a lot of fat. I drink only

_____ milk.

☐ 2. I eat a lot of junk food, like chips, cookies, and cake. I never exercise. I'm often sick. I'm very _____.

☐ 3. She doesn't talk to anyone. She's very _____.

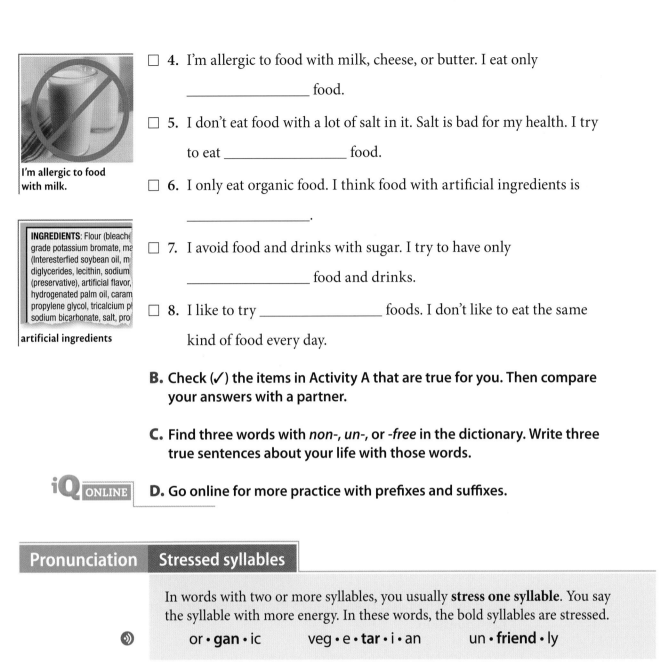

□ **4.** I'm allergic to food with milk, cheese, or butter. I eat only

_____ food.

□ **5.** I don't eat food with a lot of salt in it. Salt is bad for my health. I try

to eat _____ food.

□ **6.** I only eat organic food. I think food with artificial ingredients is

_____.

□ **7.** I avoid food and drinks with sugar. I try to have only

_____ food and drinks.

□ **8.** I like to try _____ foods. I don't like to eat the same

kind of food every day.

**I'm allergic to food with milk.**

INGREDIENTS: Flour (bleache
grade potassium bromate, ma
(Interesterfied soybean oil, m
diglycerides, lecithin, sodium
(preservative), artificial flavor,
hydrogenated palm oil, caram
propylene glycol, tricalcium pl
sodium bicarbonate, salt, pro

**artificial ingredients**

**B.** Check (✓) the items in Activity A that are true for you. Then compare
your answers with a partner.

**C.** Find three words with *non-*, *un-*, or *-free* in the dictionary. Write three
true sentences about your life with those words.

**D.** Go online for more practice with prefixes and suffixes.

---

| Pronunciation | Stressed syllables |

In words with two or more syllables, you usually **stress one syllable**. You say
the syllable with more energy. In these words, the bold syllables are stressed.

or • **gan** • ic        veg • e • **tar** • i • an        un • **friend** • ly

**A.** Listen to the words. Circle the stressed syllables. Then practice with
a partner.

1. de • li • cious
2. al • ler • gic
3. un • health • y
4. ed • u • ca • tion
5. in • gre • di • ent

6. su • gar • free
7. gar • den
8. din • ner
9. non • dai • ry
10. com • mu • ni • ty

 **B.** Listen to the sentences. Circle the stressed syllables in words with two or more syllables.

 **Tip** for Success

We usually don't stress words like pronouns, prepositions, and articles. See the Pronunciation box on page 31 for more information.

1. In my opinion, artificial ingredients are unsafe.

2. He doesn't eat chicken or beef.

3. He wants to lose weight, so he's on a diet.

4. This soup has an unusual flavor.

5. Are these cookies sugar-free?

6. She grows organic tomatoes in her garden.

**C.** Listen again. Underline the stressed words in the sentences.

**iQ ONLINE**  **D.** Go online for more practice with stressed syllables.

## Listening Skill | Listening for reasons

Speakers use reasons to explain their actions. In conversations, speakers often use **why** to ask for reasons. They use **because** to give reasons.

A: **Why** do you eat sugar-free food?     A: **Why** don't you eat fast food?

B: **Because** sugar is bad for your teeth.     B: **Because** it has artificial ingredients in it.

Listen for these two key words—*why* and *because*—to understand reasons.

**A.** Read the sentences. Then listen to the conversations. Circle the answer to each question.

1. Why does John buy only organic apples?
   a. Because they are cheap.
   b. Because they're good for him.
   c. Because he likes the flavor.
   d. Because they're sweet.

2. Why does Amanda avoid fattening foods?
   a. Because she doesn't like them.
   b. Because she wants to lose weight.
   c. Because they're bad for her health.
   d. Because she's allergic.

3. Why does James want to go out for dinner?
   a. Because his friend is a terrible cook.
   b. Because he is a terrible cook.
   c. Because it's cheap.
   d. Because he doesn't have any food at home.

fattening foods

4. Kay's Kitchen is Anna's favorite restaurant. Why?
   a. Because it's near her house.
   c. Because their food is cheap.
   b. Because their food is delicious.
   d. Because it's organic.

**B. Are you similar to John, Amanda, James, or Anna? Tell your classmates.**

*I think I'm similar to John. We both like organic food.*

 **C. Go online for more practice with listening for reasons.**

# SAY WHAT YOU THINK

**A. Answer these questions.**

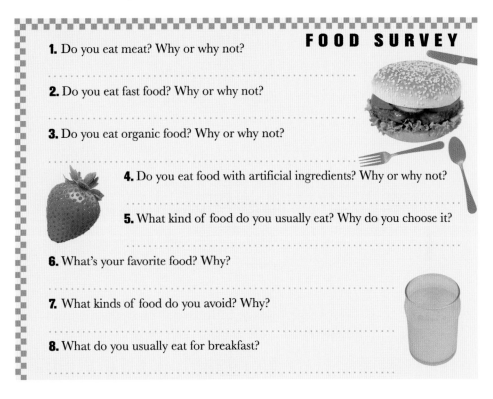

**FOOD SURVEY**

**1.** Do you eat meat? Why or why not?

**2.** Do you eat fast food? Why or why not?

**3.** Do you eat organic food? Why or why not?

**4.** Do you eat food with artificial ingredients? Why or why not?

**5.** What kind of food do you usually eat? Why do you choose it?

**6.** What's your favorite food? Why?

**7.** What kinds of food do you avoid? Why?

**8.** What do you usually eat for breakfast?

**Tip for Success**

You can use *Why don't you...?* or *Why doesn't he / she...?* to ask why someone doesn't do something.

**B. Discuss your answers with a partner.**

A: *Do you eat meat?*
B: *Yes, I do.*

A: *Why?*
B: *Because it's delicious and I like the flavor.*

# SPEAKING

**UNIT OBJECTIVE** ▶▶▶
At the end of this unit, you are going to design a survey about food and interview a classmate.

| Grammar | Verbs + gerunds or infinitives |
|---|---|

1.  Gerunds and infinitives are usually words for activities.
    - A gerund is a **base verb** + **-ing**: *eating, cooking, baking*.
    - An infinitive is **to** + **a base verb**: *to eat, to cook, to bake*.

2.  **Verbs + gerunds** You can use gerunds after these verbs.

    | subject | verb | gerund |
    |---|---|---|
    | We | **enjoy** | **cooking.** |
    | I | **avoid** | **buying** fast food. |

3.  **Verbs + infinitives** You can use infinitives after these verbs.

    | subject | verb | infinitive |
    |---|---|---|
    | He | **tries** | **to eat** only organic food. |
    | We | **need** | **to make** dinner. |
    | They | **want** | **to eat** only healthy food. |

4.  **Verbs + gerunds <u>or</u> infinitives** You can use gerunds or infinitives after these verbs.

    | subject | verb | gerund or infinitive |
    |---|---|---|
    | He | likes | **to eat** at home.<br>**eating** at home. |
    | We | hate | **to shop** at Bob's Market.<br>**shopping** at Bob's Market. |
    | They | love | **to go out** to dinner.<br>**going out** to dinner. |
    | I | can't stand | **to cook.**<br>**cooking.** |

**A. Listen to the sentences. What do you hear? Circle the gerund or infinitive.**

1. (to cook)/ cooking
2. to eat / eating
3. to shop / shopping
4. to buy / buying
5. to eat / eating
6. to avoid / avoiding
7. to cook / cooking
8. to eat / eating
9. to eat / eating
10. to go / going

**B. Complete the conversation with the correct infinitive or gerund forms. In some sentences, both a gerund and an infinitive are correct.**

**Mary:** Sun-Hee, I have to make dinner for my husband's parents on Friday night. I'm so nervous. Can you help me?

**Sun-Hee:** Sure, I love _____ (cook). What kinds of food do
                    1

they like _____ (eat)?
                 2

**Mary:** Well, my mother-in-law enjoys _____ (try) new
                                               3

things, but my father-in-law avoids _____ (eat) a lot of
                                          4

different things. For example, he's allergic to dairy foods, and he tries

_____ (avoid) foods with a lot of salt.
          5

**Sun-Hee:** What do they like?

**Mary:** Um, they like chicken and fish. And they like vegetables.

**Sun-Hee:** All right. I have a great recipe for roast chicken and vegetables.
              It's spicy, but it's not very salty.

**Mary:** That sounds perfect! Thanks so much. I try _____
                                                          6
(cook), but I'm not very good in the kitchen.

spicy

**Sun-Hee:** No problem. What time do you want _____ (start)?
                                                        7

**Mary:** How about 3:00?

**Sun-Hee:** Great! I'll see you then!

**C.** Complete the sentences with information about food. Use a verb + infinitive or gerund in each sentence. Share your ideas with a partner.

| avoid | buy | drink | feel | go | have | make |
|-------|-----|-------|------|-----|------|------|
| bake | cook | eat | find | grow | listen | tell |

1. I want *to grow a garden at home.*

2. I need _____

3. I try _____

4. I like _____

5. I love _____

6. I hate _____

**D.** Go online for more practice with verbs + gerunds or infinitives.

**E.** Go online for the grammar expansion.

---

**Unit Assignment** | Design a survey and interview a classmate

In this assignment, you are going to design a survey and interview a classmate about his or her food choices. Think about the Unit Question, "How do you choose your food?" Use the listening, the unit video, and your work in this unit. Look at the Self-Assessment checklist on page 50.

## CONSIDER THE IDEAS

Listen to the interview. Match the questions to the student's answers.

1. What's your favorite food? ____    a. Because I'm allergic to them.

2. Do you think organic food is good for you? ____    b. Nonfat yogurt.

3. Why do you avoid strawberries? ____    c. I don't know.

4. What do you usually eat for breakfast? ____    d. Because it fills me up and gives me energy.

5. Why do you choose nonfat yogurt? ____    e. Pizza.

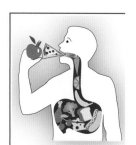

It fills me up.

# PREPARE AND SPEAK

**A.** **FIND IDEAS** **Work with a partner. Write ten interview questions.**

- Write questions about food likes, dislikes, choices, and opinions.
- Include questions with gerunds and infinitives.

**B.** **ORGANIZE IDEAS** **Work with your partner and prepare your survey.**

1. Look at your ten questions from Activity A. Circle your four best questions. Include at least one opinion question.

2. Write your questions. Leave room for answers and follow-up questions.

---

**Note-taking Skill** | **Taking notes on an interview**

Before you interview someone, write your interview questions on a piece of paper. Leave room below each question for notes and follow-up answers. Don't write complete sentences for the answers. Write only the most important words.

Read this sample from an interview.

> **Q:** What are your favorite foods?
>
> **A:** Well, I like pizza a lot. I also really like teriyaki chicken. Cherries are my favorite fruit.
>
> **Q:** What foods do you eat every day?
>
> **A:** Let's see. I eat yogurt every morning for breakfast. I also have rice with my dinner every day. Sometimes I have rice at lunchtime, too.

Look at the sample notes below. Notice the note-taker left room for notes about the speaker's answers and wrote only the most important words.

> Q:   What are your favorite foods?
>
> A:   pizza, teriyaki chicken, cherries
>
> Q:   What foods do you eat every day?
>
> A:   yogurt, rice

 **C.** Go online for more practice with taking notes on an interview.

**Tip for Success**

When you want more information, you can ask **a follow-up question**. For example: *Why is it your favorite? Why not?*

When you are answering an interviewer's questions, remember to use the phrases *In my opinion*, and *I think that* to give your opinion. Review the Speaking Skill box in Unit 2 on page 32.

**D. SPEAK** Follow these steps. Look at the Self-Assessment checklist below before you begin.

1. Each partner works individually. Use the questions to interview another student in your class. Take notes on his or her answers.

**Critical Thinking Tip**

Activity C asks you to tell the class about your answers. You have to **summarize** the information. This shows you understand the ideas.

2. Look over your notes. Are they clear? Make changes and add words to make your notes clearer.

3. Work with your partner. Check your notes. Did you write your partner's answers correctly?

4. Compare your answers with your partner's answers. How are the answers the same or different? Share your ideas with the class.

**iQ ONLINE** Go online for your alternate Unit Assignment.

## CHECK AND REFLECT

**A. CHECK** Think about the Unit Assignment as you complete the Self-Assessment checklist.

| SELF-ASSESSMENT | | |
|---|---|---|
| Yes | No | |
| ☐ | ☐ | Our interview questions were clear. |
| ☐ | ☐ | I used vocabulary from this unit. |
| ☐ | ☐ | I used gerunds and infinitives correctly. |
| ☐ | ☐ | I gave reasons for my opinions when answering questions. |

**B. REFLECT** Go to the Online Discussion Board to discuss these questions.

1. What is something new you learned in this unit?

2. Think about the Unit Question—How do you choose your food? Is your answer different now than when you started this unit? If yes, how is it different? Why?

# TRACK YOUR SUCCESS

**Circle the words you have learned in this unit.**

**Nouns**
flavor 🔑
ingredient
vegetarian

**Adjectives**
nondairy
nonfat
nutritious
organic
salt-free
social 🔑
sugar-free
unfriendly 🔑

unhealthy
unsafe
unusual 🔑

**Verbs**
avoid 🔑
bake 🔑
buy 🔑
cook 🔑
drink 🔑
eat 🔑
enjoy 🔑
feel 🔑
find 🔑
go 🔑

grow 🔑
hate 🔑
have 🔑
like 🔑
listen 🔑
love 🔑
make 🔑
need 🔑
(can't) stand
start 🔑
tell 🔑
try 🔑
want 🔑

**Conjunction**
because 🔑

🔑 Oxford 2000 keywords
**AWL** Academic Word List

**Check (✓) the skills you learned. If you need more work on a skill, refer to the page(s) in parentheses.**

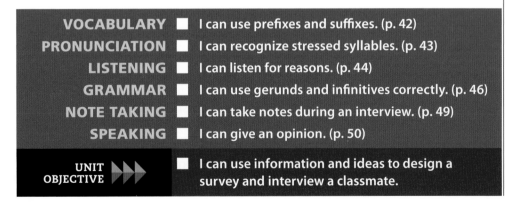

| | |
|---|---|
| **VOCABULARY** ☐ | I can use prefixes and suffixes. (p. 42) |
| **PRONUNCIATION** ☐ | I can recognize stressed syllables. (p. 43) |
| **LISTENING** ☐ | I can listen for reasons. (p. 44) |
| **GRAMMAR** ☐ | I can use gerunds and infinitives correctly. (p. 46) |
| **NOTE TAKING** ☐ | I can take notes during an interview. (p. 49) |
| **SPEAKING** ☐ | I can give an opinion. (p. 50) |
| **UNIT OBJECTIVE** ▶▶▶ ☐ | I can use information and ideas to design a survey and interview a classmate. |

UNIT 4

| NOTE TAKING | ▶ | taking notes on reasons |
| LISTENING | ▶ | review: listening for reasons |
| VOCABULARY | ▶ | collocations with *do*, *play*, and *go* |
| GRAMMAR | ▶ | subject and object pronouns |
| PRONUNCIATION | ▶ | reduced pronouns |
| SPEAKING | ▶ | agreeing and disagreeing |

Sociology

**UNIT QUESTION**

# What makes something fun?

**A** Discuss these questions with your classmates.

1. Complete the chart. Then compare charts with a partner.

| What is... | |
| --- | --- |
| a fun activity? | |
| a boring activity? | |
| an exciting activity? | |
| a dangerous activity? | |
| an interesting activity? | |

2. Look at the photo. Describe what the person is doing. Why do people do this type of activity?

**B** Listen to *The Q Classroom* online. Then answer these questions.

1. What did the students say? What are some things they like to do?

2. Do you like the same things that they like?

**C** Go to the Online Discussion Board to discuss the Unit Question with your classmates.

UNIT
OBJECTIVE ▶▶▶ Listen to a travel report. Use information and ideas to
have a group discussion about fun places in your area.

Remember: In conversations, speakers give reasons to explain their activities. They ask for reasons with **why**. They use words like **because** and **because of** to show they are giving a reason. After *because*, use a complete sentence. After *because of*, use a noun or noun phrase.

**Why** do you go to the mall?

I go to the mall **because** <u>there are a lot of great shops!</u>

I go to the mall **because of** <u>the great shops!</u>

Use a T-chart to take notes about activities and reasons. The T-chart below shows an activity and a reason for the example sentences above. A T-chart can help you organize your ideas.

| Activity | Reasons |
|---|---|
| go to the mall | a lot of great shops |

**A.** Listen to two students talking in a shopping mall. Then complete the T-chart below with activities and reasons.

| Activity | Reasons |
|---|---|
| the man comes to the mall | 1. <u>to buy clothes</u> |
|  | 2. _____ |
|  | 3. _____ |
|  | 4. _____ |
| the woman comes to the mall | 5. _____ |
|  | 6. _____ |

 **B.** Go online for more practice with taking notes on reasons.

# LISTENING

**UNIT OBJECTIVE** ▶▶▶

You are going to listen to an interview about a famous park. Think about what makes something fun.

## PREVIEW THE LISTENING

**A.** **VOCABULARY** Here are some words from the listening. Read these sentences. Then complete the sentences on page 56 with the underlined words.

**Vocabulary Skill Review**

In Unit 2, you learned about using the dictionary to find antonyms. Can you find antonyms for the vocabulary words *modern*, *outdoors*, *crowded*, and *relaxing*?

Tom likes <u>modern</u> literature.

Toshi loves to look at <u>architecture</u>.

Do you want to go to an <u>exhibition</u>?

In the summer, we sometimes eat <u>outdoors</u>.

There is a great hiking <u>path</u> in the woods near my house.

Sun-Hee likes to be in <u>nature</u>. She loves trees and flowers.

James doesn't like <u>crowded</u> streets. There are too many people!

Keith likes to read on the weekend. It's very <u>relaxing</u>.

1. I like to read a book in the evening. It's _____.

2. I don't like _____ cars. I like older cars.

3 There are a lot of people here! It's really _____.

4. Let's walk on my favorite _____ in the park. It goes around the lake.

5. I love to spend time in _____. I like to look at the trees, the grass, and the animals.

6. This _____ is really great! I love to visit museums.

7. I like to play basketball _____. I don't like to play in a gym.

8. I like the _____ in Dubai, especially the tall buildings.

**B.** Go online for more practice with the vocabulary.

**C.** **PREVIEW** You are going to listen to a reporter talk about Ibirapuera Park (pronounced *ee-BIH-ra-poo-AIR-ah*), a large park in the city of São Paulo, Brazil.

São Paulo, Brazil

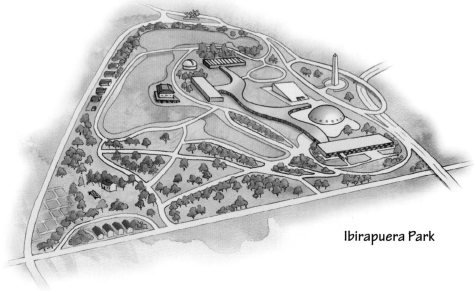
Ibirapuera Park

Check (✓) the places you think are in Ibirapuera Park.

☐ a beach    ☐ a lake    ☐ paths    ☐ a shopping mall
☐ a museum   ☐ a library  ☐ roads    ☐ sports fields
☐ gardens    ☐ museums    ☐ architecture  ☐ a swimming pool

# WORK WITH THE LISTENING

**A.** Look at the list of places. Check (✓) the things that are in Ibirapuera Park. Then compare your answers with a partner. How many of your predictions were correct?

☐ architecture      ☐ hiking paths      ☐ roads

☐ a beach      ☐ a lake      ☐ a shopping mall

☐ food stalls      ☐ a library      ☐ sports fields

☐ gardens      ☐ museums      ☐ a swimming pool

| Skill Review | Listening for reasons |
| --- | --- |

Remember: In conversations, speakers often use *why* to ask for reasons. They use *because* to give reasons. Review the Listening Skill box in Unit 3 on page 44.

**B.** **LISTEN AND TAKE NOTES** Listen again to the students talking about why they like Ibirapuera Park. Then complete the chart.

| Activity | Reasons |
| --- | --- |
| Isabel comes to the park. | She thinks it's fun. |
| Carlos comes to the park. | |

**C.** Read the questions. Circle the correct answer.

1. What does Isabel like to look at in the park?
   a. the trees
   b. the gardens
   c. the important buildings
   d. the beautiful structures

2. Why does Isabel like the food stalls?
   a. They're delicious and they're outdoors.
   b. The food is cheap.
   c. They're in the Museum of Modern History.
   d. She tries new food each time.

3. What does Carlos <u>not</u> do in the park?
   a. go hiking on the paths
   b. go swimming in a lake
   c. ride his bike
   d. enjoy spending time in nature

4. What does Carlos like to look at?
   a. the trees and gardens
   b. the important buildings
   c. the city around the park
   d. the beautiful structures

 **D.** Go online to listen to *Where Do You Like to Go for Vacation?* and check your comprehension.

iQ ONLINE

## Building Vocabulary  Collocations with *do*, *play*, and *go*

**Words for activities** often follow the verbs *do*, *play*, or *go*.

> They **do gymnastics** on Saturdays.
> She **plays basketball** at her school.
> He **goes skiing** in the mountains.

| Do | Play | Go* |
|---|---|---|
| do aerobics | play baseball | go hiking |
| do crosswords | play Scrabble | go jogging |
| do gymnastics | play soccer | go shopping |
| do judo | play tennis | go skiing |
| do nothing | play video games | go swimming |

*You usually use the verb *go* with a gerund (verb + *-ing*).

**Tip for Success**

The word *let's* introduces suggestions.

**A.** Complete the conversations with *play*, *do*, or *go*.

1. **Sara:** Emma, I'm bored. Let's do something.

   **Emma:** Sure. Let's _____ shopping.

   **Sara:** I don't like shopping. Let's _____ video games.

   **Emma:** No, I'm not good at video games. Uh, do you want to

   _____ hiking?

   **Sara:** OK. That's a great idea!

shopping

2. **John:** Mike, I want to lose weight. What do you do for exercise?

   **Mike:** I _____ judo. I have a class twice a week.

   **John:** Do you still _____ gymnastics?

   **Mike:** No, it was too difficult.

judo

3. **Sandra:** Mei, do you want to _____ swimming with me?

   **Mei:** No, thanks. I have training.

   **Sandra:** Oh, do you _____ a sport?

   **Mei:** Yes, I _____ soccer. Hey, do you want to

   _____ skiing this weekend?

   **Sandra:** Sure, that sounds like fun!

skiing

Critical Thinking **Tip**

In Activity B,
you **practice** the
collocations. This
helps you remember
vocabulary better.

**B.** Answer the questions with information about yourself. Include the verbs *play*, *do*, or *go* in every sentence. Then ask and answer the questions with a partner.

1. **A:** What do you like to do on weekends?

   **B:** I like to _____.

2. **A:** What do you like to do at night?

   **B:** I like to _____.

3. **A:** What else do you like to do for fun?

   **B:** I like to _____.

4. **A:** What do you hate to do?

   **B:** I really hate to _____.

**iQ ONLINE** **C.** Go online for more practice with collocations with *do*, *play*, and *go*.

# SAY WHAT YOU THINK

**A.** Give your opinion about fun. Circle *Yes* or *No* for each sentence.

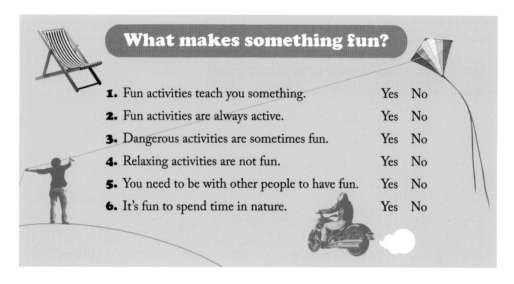

**What makes something fun?**

| | | | |
|---|---|---|---|
| **1.** | Fun activities teach you something. | Yes | No |
| **2.** | Fun activities are always active. | Yes | No |
| **3.** | Dangerous activities are sometimes fun. | Yes | No |
| **4.** | Relaxing activities are not fun. | Yes | No |
| **5.** | You need to be with other people to have fun. | Yes | No |
| **6.** | It's fun to spend time in nature. | Yes | No |

**B.** Discuss the questions with a group.

1. What is your favorite park? Why is it your favorite?

2. Why are parks important?

**C.** Go online to watch a video about a special park in New York City. Then check your comprehension.

> **VIDEO VOCABULARY**
>
> **garden** *(n.)* a place for growing flowers or vegetables
> **ground** *(n.)* the surface of the Earth
> **tourist** *(n.)* a person who visits a place on vacation
> **track** *(n.)* long lines of metal that trains ride on

**D.** Think about the video and the listening as you discuss these questions.

1. Which park do you want to go to? Why?

2. How are the two parks different? How are they the same?

3. Are these parks fun places? Why or why not?

 **UNIT OBJECTIVE** ▶▶▶ At the end of this unit, you are going to have a group discussion about fun places in your area.

| Grammar | Subject and object pronouns |

1. Subjects and objects can be nouns.
   - Subjects come before verbs in statements.
   - Objects come after verbs or prepositions, like *at*, *in*, and *on*.

| subject | verb | object | preposition + object |
|---|---|---|---|
| **Kate** | likes | the **book**. | |
| My **brother** | runs | — | in the **park**. |

2. Pronouns replace nouns.
   - You use some pronouns for subjects.
   - You use other pronouns for objects.

| | subject pronoun | object pronoun |
|---|---|---|
| singular | **I** have a great soccer coach. | He helps **me**. |
| | **You** are good at swimming. | I want to go with **you**. |
| | **He** goes hiking a lot. | I sometimes see **him** in the park. |
| | **She** is good at math. | I like studying with **her**. |
| | I like the park. **It's** really big. | My friends like **it** too. |
| plural | **We** go shopping on Sundays. | Our friends meet **us** at the mall. |
| | **You** play baseball a lot. | I sometimes see **you** at the field. |
| | **They** are great soccer players. | I like to watch **them**. |

3. You usually use pronouns *he / him*, *she / her*, *it / it*, *we / us*, and *they / them* after you know the noun.

   Mary has a brother named Tom. **She** studies with **him** every Friday.

   (Mary = **she**; Tom = **him**)

**A.** Circle the correct pronoun.

1. ( He / Him ) goes hiking on Saturdays.

2. Let's go to the mall with ( they / them ) tomorrow.

3. ( We / Us ) like to spend time at the park.

4. Sarah's friends make ( she / her ) laugh.

5. I like this flower. ( He / It ) is beautiful.

6. John and ( I / me ) love to play tennis.

7. James plays baseball with Sam and ( I / me ).

8. Fun activities sometimes teach ( we / us ) something.

**B.** Complete each sentence with a pronoun for the underlined word.

1. That TV <u>show</u> is really exciting. I watch _____ every week.

2. Isabel's <u>sister</u> loves to go hiking. _____ goes every weekend.

3. The free <u>exhibitions</u> are wonderful. I really love _____.

4. I see my <u>grandmother</u> on Wednesdays. I have lunch with _____.

5. My <u>classes</u> are very interesting, but _____ are difficult.

6. <u>Faisal and Miteb</u> go jogging in the park. Then _____ have lunch.

7. <u>We</u> play basketball in the gym. Sometimes, our friends join _____.

8. I want to play tennis with <u>you</u>. _____ are an excellent player.

jogging

**C.** Look back at Activities A and B. Write an *S* over all the subject pronouns. Write an *O* over all the object pronouns.

**D.** Complete the conversation with the correct subject and object pronouns.

**Sarah:** Maria, how do _____ like your cooking class?
1

**Maria:** I love _____! My teacher is great. She's from
2

France, and _____ really knows how to cook. What's
3

new with you?

**Sarah:** I'm taking a writing class.

**Maria:** Oh, do _____ write stories?
4

**Sarah:** No, but _____ write poetry. The class is really fun. I
5

like the other students. _____ are very talented.
6

**Maria:** That's great. Hey, my friends and I are going to the beach

this weekend. Do _____ want to come with
7

_____?
8

**Sarah:** Sure, that sounds fun and relaxing.

beach

**E.** Go online for more practice with subject and object pronouns.

**F.** Go online for the grammar expansion.

---

| Pronunciation | Reduced pronouns |
|---|---|

You usually say pronouns quickly, with no stress. When you say *he, him, her,*
and *them,* you don't usually pronounce the beginning sounds. You "**reduce**"
the words.

I think **he's** at the park.          I don't see **him.**
Is that **her** bike?          Let's call **them.**

You <u>do</u> pronounce the "h" of *he* when it's the first word in a sentence.

**He's** at the park.

**A. Complete the conversations with *he*, *him*, *her*, and *them*. Then listen and check your answers. Practice the conversations with a partner. Say the reduced forms.**

1. **A:** John is a fun guy. How do you know _____? Does

   _____ play soccer with you?

   **B:** No. I know _____ from school. How do you know

   _____?

   **A:** _____ spends time at the park near my house. Sometimes

   _____ plays basketball there with my friends and me.

2. **A:** Anna's sister Emma is here this weekend. Do you know

   _____?

   **B:** Yes, I do. I really like _____.

   **A:** Me too. Do you think Anna and Emma want to go for a walk

   with us this afternoon?

   **B:** Maybe. Let's call _____.

**B. Write four sentences with *he*, *him*, *her*, and *them*. Then take turns reading your sentences with a partner.**

1. _____

2. _____

3. _____

4. _____

 **C. Go online for more practice with reduced pronouns.**

Use these expressions to **agree** with another person's opinion.

| Agreeing with a positive opinion | Agreeing with a negative opinion |
|---|---|
| **A:** I like swimming. <br> **B:** I do too. / Me too.* | **A:** I don't like swimming. <br> **B:** I don't either. / Me neither.* |

*  *Me too* and *Me neither* sound more informal.

Use these expressions to **disagree** with another person's opinion. These expressions sound more friendly or polite.

| Disagreeing politely | |
|---|---|
| **A:** I think that the building is pretty. <br> **B:** Oh, I don't know. | **A:** I love that park. How about you? <br> **B:** I'm not sure. |

I do too.

I'm not sure.

**A.** Listen to the short conversations. Check (✓) *Agree* or *Disagree* for each conversation. Then listen again and write the expression that you hear.

| | Agree | Disagree | Expression |
|---|---|---|---|
| **1.** | ☐ | ☐ | |
| **2.** | ☐ | ☐ | |
| **3.** | ☐ | ☐ | |
| **4.** | ☐ | ☐ | |
| **5.** | ☐ | ☐ | |
| **6.** | ☐ | ☐ | |

**B.** Write six sentences about things that you like or don't like. Then read them to a partner. Your partner will agree or disagree.

1. I really like _____.

2. I don't like _____.

3. I think _____.

4. I think _____.

5. I enjoy _____.

4. I hate _____.

**iQ** ONLINE **C.** Go online for more practice with agreeing and disagreeing.

---

**Unit Assignment**   **Have a group discussion about fun places in your area**

UNIT OBJECTIVE ▶▶▶  In this assignment, you are going to have a group discussion about the "top five" fun places in your area. Think about the unit question, "What makes something fun?" Use the listening, the unit video, and your work in this unit. Look at the Self-Assessment checklist on page 68.

## CONSIDER THE IDEAS

**A.** Listen to a group discuss the fun places in their area. What places do they talk about? Check (✓) the six places. Then compare with a partner.

☐ the city park ☐ the Modern History Museum

☐ the swimming pool ☐ the shopping mall

☐ the library ☐ the beach

☐ the gym ☐ downtown

☐ hiking trails ☐ a garden

**B.** Do you agree with the answers in Activity A? Are they fun places? Which places do you think are fun? Discuss your answers with a partner.

# PREPARE AND SPEAK

**A.** FIND IDEAS What are your five favorite places in your area? Complete the chart with your ideas. Give reasons for each place.

| | Name of fun place | Why is it a fun place? |
|---|---|---|
| 1. | | |
| 2. | | |
| 3. | | |
| 4. | | |
| 5. | | |

**Tip for Success**

You can share ideas and give suggestions with the expressions *How about…?* and *What about…?*

**B.** ORGANIZE IDEAS Choose three ideas from Activity A. Practice different ways to share your ideas. You can use these phrases.

*I think that the park is a really fun place because there's a lake.*

*How about the park? It has hiking paths.*

**C.** SPEAK Work with a group. Discuss your ideas. Look at the Self-Assessment checklist below before you begin.

- Share your three places and your reasons.
- Listen carefully to others' ideas. Agree or disagree with them.
- As a group, choose the best five places.

 Go online for your alternate Unit Assignment.

# CHECK AND REFLECT

**A.** CHECK Think about the Unit Assignment as you complete the Self-Assessment checklist.

| SELF-ASSESSMENT | | |
|---|---|---|
| Yes | No | |
| ☐ | ☐ | My information was clear. |
| ☐ | ☐ | I used vocabulary from this unit. |
| ☐ | ☐ | I made notes using a T-chart. |
| ☐ | ☐ | I used subject and object pronouns correctly. |
| ☐ | ☐ | I used expressions for agreeing and disagreeing. |
| ☐ | ☐ | I used reduced words correctly. |

**B.** **REFLECT** Go to the Online Discussion Board to discuss these questions.

1. What is something new you learned in this unit?

2. Think about the Unit Question—What makes something fun? Is your answer different now than when you started this unit? If yes, how is it different? Why?

# TRACK YOUR SUCCESS

**Circle the words and phrases you have learned in this unit.**

**Nouns**
architecture
exhibition AWL
nature 🔑
path 🔑

**Adjectives**
crowded
modern 🔑
relaxing 🔑 AWL

**Adverb**
outdoors

**Collocations**
do aerobics

do crosswords
do gymnastics
do judo
do nothing
go hiking
go jogging
go shopping
go skiing
go swimming
play baseball
play basketball
play Scrabble
play soccer
play video games

**Phrases**
I do too.
I don't either.
I'm not sure.
Me neither.
Me too.
Oh, I don't know.

**Pronouns**
he - him 🔑
I - me 🔑
it - it 🔑
she - her 🔑
they - them 🔑
we - us 🔑
you - you 🔑

🔑 Oxford 2000 keywords
AWL Academic Word List

**Check (✓) the skills you learned. If you need more work on a skill, refer to the page(s) in parentheses.**

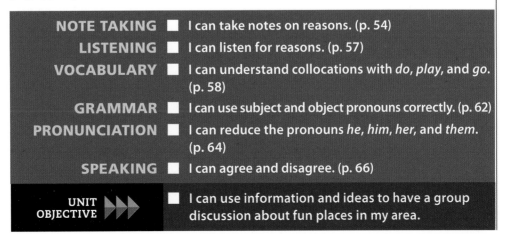

| | |
|---|---|
| NOTE TAKING | ☐ I can take notes on reasons. (p. 54) |
| LISTENING | ☐ I can listen for reasons. (p. 57) |
| VOCABULARY | ☐ I can understand collocations with *do*, *play*, and *go*. (p. 58) |
| GRAMMAR | ☐ I can use subject and object pronouns correctly. (p. 62) |
| PRONUNCIATION | ☐ I can reduce the pronouns *he*, *him*, *her*, and *them*. (p. 64) |
| SPEAKING | ☐ I can agree and disagree. (p. 66) |
| UNIT OBJECTIVE ▶▶▶ | ☐ I can use information and ideas to have a group discussion about fun places in my area. |

UNIT **5**

Architecture

| LISTENING | ▶ | listening for opinions |
| NOTE TAKING | ▶ | taking notes on pros and cons |
| VOCABULARY | ▶ | compound nouns |
| PRONUNCIATION | ▶ | stress in compound nouns |
| GRAMMAR | ▶ | prepositions of location |
| SPEAKING | ▶ | review: agreeing and disagreeing |

**Q ?**

### UNIT QUESTION

# What makes a good home?

**A** Discuss these questions with your classmates.

1. Which words are places to live? Circle them. Add two more places.

| apartment | house | park |
| dormitory | mansion | restaurant |
| garage | office | studio |
| hotel | _____ | _____ |

2. Use two adjectives to describe your home.

3. Look at the photos. Describe each place. What makes each one a good place to live?

**B** Listen to *The Q Classroom* online. Match the ideas from the box to the students. Then answer the questions.

a.  A good home is quiet.

b.  I want to be right next to the beach.

c.  ~~My roommates are nice.~~

d.  Location is important.

| What makes a good home? |
|---|
| Yuna | *c. My roommates are nice.* |
| Felix | |
| Marcus | |
| Sophy | |

1.  What are some good things about living with roommates? About living alone?

2.  When you choose a home, is location important to you? What else is important?

iQ ONLINE

**C** Go to the Online Discussion Board to discuss the Unit Question with your classmates.

# LISTENING

## LISTENING 1 | How Do You Like Your Home?

**UNIT OBJECTIVE** ▶▶▶ You are going to listen to a conversation about choosing a home. Think about what makes a good home.

### PREVIEW THE LISTENING

**A.** **VOCABULARY** Here are some words from Listening 1. Read the sentences. Which explanation is correct? Circle *a* or *b*.

1. Rob watches loud TV shows. His apartment is <u>noisy</u>.
   a. Rob's apartment is quiet.
   b. Rob's apartment isn't quiet.

2. Marta likes her <u>private</u> room, but she sometimes gets lonely.
   a. Marta doesn't share her room with someone.
   b. Marta shares her room with someone.

3. Matt's apartment is in a great <u>location</u>. It's on a quiet street near his school.
   a. His apartment is cheap and very large.
   b. His apartment is in a convenient place.

4. Sara has a <u>comfortable</u> chair. She likes to sit in it.
   a. The chair is very soft.
   b. The chair is very hard.

5. David's <u>rent</u> is really expensive, so he wants to get a roommate.
   a. David's apartment is free.
   b. David pays a lot of money for his apartment.

6. Jamal and Saud are <u>roommates</u>. They both live in Room 215.
   a. Jamal and Saud live together.
   b. Jamal and Saud have a class together.

7. Walaa lives with her <u>extended family</u>, including her parents, her grandmother and grandfather, and two cousins.
   a. Walaa lives with many family members.
   b. Walaa lives with some friends from school.

🔑 Oxford 2000 keywords

**8.** Our city doesn't have <u>public transportation</u>. People usually walk or drive.

    a. The city has no streets or sidewalks.

    b. The city has no buses or trains.

 **B.** Go online for more practice with the vocabulary.

 **C.** **PREVIEW** You are going to listen to Amanda talk to her classmates. She wants to move closer to school, and she wants some advice.

Write two good things about your home and two bad things about your home.

*I like my roommates.*           *My apartment is noisy.*

**Good:** _____

_____

**Bad:** _____

_____

# WORK WITH THE LISTENING

**A.** Listen to the three conversations. Write the correct name below each picture. Does the person like his or her home? Check (✓) *Likes* or *Dislikes*.

| Carlos | John | Mary |
|---|---|---|

1. _____

☐ Likes

☐ Dislikes

2. _____

☐ Likes

☐ Dislikes

3. _____

☐ Likes

☐ Dislikes

**B.** Look at these statements. Which are good points and which are bad points? Write each statement in the correct part of the chart.

| The rent is expensive. | It's far from school. |
|---|---|
| I don't pay any rent. | It's near public transportation. |
| It's noisy. | I like the people I live with. |
| It's comfortable. | It's not private. |
| It's near school and classes. | It's near coffee shops and stores. |

|  | John | Mary | Carlos |
|---|---|---|---|
| **Good Points:** | | | |
| 1. | ☐ | ☐ | ☐ |
| 2. | ☐ | ☐ | ☐ |
| 3. | ☐ | ☐ | ☐ |
| 4. | ☐ | ☐ | ☐ |
| 5. | ☐ | ☐ | ☐ |
| 6. | ☐ | ☐ | ☐ |
| **Bad Points:** | | | |
| 7. | ☐ | ☐ | ☐ |
| 8. | ☐ | ☐ | ☐ |
| 9. | ☐ | ☐ | ☐ |
| 10. | ☐ | ☐ | ☐ |

**C.** Listen again. Check (✓) the correct name for each point in the chart. You will check some items more than once.

**D.** Circle the best answer to each question.

1. Which statement best describes John's home?
   a. It has a good location, but the people are not friendly.
   b. It's small and noisy, but the people are nice.
   c. The location is good, but it's expensive.
   d. It's far from school, but it has a garage for his car.

2. Which statement best describes Mary's home?
   a. It's small, and it's in a bad location.
   b. It's far from school, but it's close to public transportation.
   c. It's close to school, but it's in a dangerous neighborhood.
   d. It's in a good location, but it's expensive.

3. Which statement best describes Carlos's home?
   a. It's free, and he lives alone.
   b. It's in a good location, but it's expensive.
   c. It's free, and it's close public transportation.
   d. It's noisy and crowded, but it's close to school.

4. What does Amanda want?
   a. a cheap apartment close to school
   b. an expensive apartment close to public transportation
   c. a small apartment close to work
   d. a large apartment with a lot of roommates

**E.** How is your home similar to or different from the speakers' homes? Complete the chart.

|  | Similarities to my home | Differences from my home |
|---|---|---|
| **John's home** |  |  |
| **Mary's home** |  |  |
| **Carlos's home** |  |  |

**F.** Which home do you like: John's, Mary's, or Carlos's? Why?

I like _____'s home because…

**G.** Go online to listen to *Choosing a House* and check your comprehension.

# SAY WHAT YOU THINK

**A.** Read the sentences. What is important to you? Check (✓) five sentences. Then rank them from 1 to 5. (Put a *1* next to the most important thing.)

**Critical Thinking** Tip

In Activity A, you **rank** items. Ranking helps you think about what is important to you.

## what Do You Want in a Home?

- [ ] ___ I want to live in a convenient location, near stores and restaurants.
- [ ] ___ I don't want to pay a lot of rent.
- [ ] ___ I want a private room.
- [ ] ___ I want to live with my extended family.
- [ ] ___ I want to live with good friends.
- [ ] ___ I want to have nice neighbors.
- [ ] ___ I want a home near public transportation.
- [ ] ___ I want to live near a garden or park.

**B.** Work with a partner. Compare your answers in Activity A. Do you and your partner agree or disagree?

## Listening Skill | Listening for opinions

An **opinion** is something that a person thinks or feels. Speakers sometimes use *I think (that)* when they give an opinion.

**I think that** this house is very beautiful.    **I think** the location is very good.

Sometimes speakers give opinions with the words they choose. Listen for verbs (*like*, *love*, and *hate*), adjectives (*cheap*, *expensive*, *beautiful*, and *ugly*) or the word *only*.

**I love** this apartment.        It's **expensive**.

The rent is **only** $400 a month. (= I think that the rent is low.)

**A.** Listen to the conversations. What opinions do you hear? Check (✓) them.

1. Rob and Sam look at an apartment.
   - ☐ Rob and Sam like the location.
   - ☐ They think the apartment is too far from school.
   - ☐ They think that the rent is expensive.
   - ☐ They think the rent is good.

2. Mary talks to her mother.
   - ☐ Mary likes taking the bus.
   - ☐ Mary doesn't like taking the bus.
   - ☐ Mary likes her neighbors.
   - ☐ Mary doesn't like her neighbors.

3. Matt visits James's new house.
   - ☐ Matt likes James's new house.
   - ☐ Matt doesn't like James's new house.
   - ☐ James thinks that there are a lot of bedrooms.
   - ☐ James thinks that there aren't a lot of bedrooms.

4. Kate gets a new apartment.
   - ☐ Kate likes the living room in her new apartment.
   - ☐ Kate doesn't like the living room in her new apartment.
   - ☐ Mika thinks the apartment is in a good location.
   - ☐ Mika thinks the apartment is in a bad location.

**iQ** ONLINE **B.** Go online for more practice with listening for opinions.

## Note-taking Skill | Taking notes on pros and cons

When you are listening to people talk about the pros (good things) and cons (bad things) about a topic, you can use a T-chart to take notes. Remember to write only the important words in your notes.

Read this sample from a conversation.

> A: So, how do you like your new apartment?
>
> B: Well, it's in a great location. It's close to school. Also, the rent is cheap.
>
> A: That sounds great.
>
> B: Yeah. I really like my roommates, too. The only problem is there's one bathroom for four people!

Look at the notes below. Notice the note-taker wrote the pros on one side of the chart and the cons on the other side.

| Pros | Cons |
|------|------|
| good location | one bathroom, four people |
| cheap rent | |
| likes roommates | |

**A.** Listen again to Listening 1. Complete the T-chart with the pros and cons for John's home. Look at Activity B on page 74 to help you.

| Pros | Cons |
|------|------|
| | |

  **B.** Go online for more practice with taking notes on pros and cons.

# LISTENING 2 | Housing Problems, Housing Solutions

**UNIT OBJECTIVE** ▶▶▶▶ You are going to listen to a town meeting about building housing for students. Think about what makes a good home.

## PREVIEW THE LISTENING

**A. VOCABULARY** Here are some words from Listening 2. Read the definitions. Then complete the sentences below.

> **affordable** (*adjective*) not expensive
>
> **condition** (*noun*) 🔑 something in good condition is not damaged or broken
>
> **demand** (*noun*) 🔑 a need or want
>
> **entertainment** (*noun*) 🔑 fun or free-time activities
>
> **housing** (*noun*) apartments, houses, and homes
>
> **increase** (*verb*) 🔑 to become bigger
>
> **landlord** (*noun*) a person—he or she rents homes to people for money
>
> **shortage** (*noun*) not enough of something

🔑 Oxford 2000 keywords

**Vocabulary Skill Review**

In Unit 4, you learned about collocations with *do*, *play*, and *go*. Look at the sentences in Activity A. Can you find any collocations with *play*?

1. This house is in bad _____. There are holes in the walls, and it has two broken windows.

2. I have to talk to my _____. The lock on my front door is broken. I want him to fix it.

3. This apartment isn't _____. It's just too expensive!

4. We are having a water _____. People need to save water.

5. _____ in this area is a big problem. There aren't enough apartments or houses.

6. Rents _____ every year. I have to pay two percent more this year.

7. There is a big _____ for dormitory rooms this year. Everyone wants to live in the dorms.

8. Video games are my favorite type of _____. I try to play video games every weekend.

**B.** Go online for more practice with the vocabulary.

**C.** **PREVIEW**  You are going to listen to Dr. Ross Chan. He is at a town meeting. He wants the city of Jackson to build more housing for students.

Read the sentences below. Check (✓) the possible problems.

☐ There are not many dormitories.

☐ Many apartments aren't affordable for students.

☐ Some cheap apartments are near entertainment, like restaurants.

☐ Some apartments are near the campus and in safe areas.

☐ Rents are not increasing.

☐ Some inexpensive housing is in bad condition.

# WORK WITH THE LISTENING

**A.** Listen to Dr. Chan. He mentions three housing choices for students. What are they? Circle the correct letters.

a. Students can live in cheap apartments downtown.

b. They can live with many friends in a house.

c. They can live in cheap hotel rooms.

d. They can go to a different university.

e. They can live at home with their families.

**B.** Complete the notes. Write your answers from Activity A on the lines. Then write the pros and cons for each housing choice in the T-chart.

Housing choice 1: _____

| Pros | Cons |
|------|------|
|      |      |

Housing choice 2: _____

| Pros | Cons |
|------|------|
|      |      |

Housing choice 3: _____

| Pros | Cons |
|------|------|
|      |      |

**C.** Read the statements. Listen again. Write *T* (true) or *F* (false). Then correct each false statement to make it true.

_____ 1.  The new campus is large.

_____ 2.  There are a lot of fun things to do downtown.

_____ 3.  The apartments downtown are not in good condition.

_____ 4.  More people want to live downtown.

_____ 5.  The neighborhoods near campus are safe.

_____ 6.  All students can live with their families.

_____ 7.  The new university can increase business in Jackson.

_____ 8.  The city doesn't want the university to grow.

the city of Jackson

 **SAY WHAT YOU THINK**

**A.** Look at the pros and cons in your T-charts in Activity B on page 81. Which housing choice do you think is the best? Why? Write three reasons. Then discuss your answer with a partner.

Best choice: _____

Reason 1: _____

Reason 2: _____

Reason 3: _____

**iQ** ONLINE

**B.** Go online to watch the video about recycled homes. Then check your comprehension.

**empty** *(adj.)* having nothing or nobody inside

**green construction** *(n. phr.)* building things in a way that helps the environment

**recycled** *(adj.)* used again

**C.** Think about the video, Listening 1, and Listening 2 and discuss these questions.

1. What are the three most important things for a home?

2. What are three possible problems with a home?

3. Do you think the buildings in the video would be a good solution for the city of Jackson? Why or why not?

## Building Vocabulary | Compound nouns

**Compound nouns** are two-word nouns. The first noun is like an adjective. It describes the second noun. You write some compound nouns as one word and some as two words.

> **One word:** bathtub, streetcar, backyard
> **Two words:** shopping mall, police officer, public transportation

**A.** Read the sentences. Circle the compound nouns.

1. He parks his car in the driveway, not in the garage.

2. The apartment has three bedrooms and two bathrooms.

3. There is a swimming pool in the backyard.

4. They like to sit by the fireplace and read.

5. She doesn't have a mailbox, so she gets her mail from the post office.

He parks in the driveway.

6. I need to buy a smoke alarm for the living room.

7. There is a drugstore near my home.

8. There is a bookshelf in the dining room.

**B.** Read the definitions. Then write a compound noun from the Building Vocabulary box or from Activity A on page 83.

**B.** Read the definitions. Then write a compound noun from the Building Vocabulary box or from Activity A on page 83.

or from Activity A on page 83.

**Tip for Success**

To make a plural compound noun, add an -s to the end of the compound noun. Don't add an -s to the first word in the noun. Correct: *post offices* Incorrect: *posts offices*

1. _____ People get their mail from this place.

2. _____ People put their books in this.

3. _____ You can park your car here.

4. _____ You burn wood in it for heat.

5. _____ This is an open area behind a house.

6. _____ You buy medicine here.

7. _____ You can buy clothes, books, and other items here.

8. _____ This is a kind of transportation in a city.

**iQ ONLINE**  **C.** Go online for more practice with compound nouns.

| Pronunciation | Stress in compound nouns |
| --- | --- |

In compound nouns, the stress is usually on the **first** word of the compound.

**post** office          **book**shelf          **drug**store

**A.** Listen to the compound nouns. The speaker will say each compound noun twice. Which pronunciation is correct? Circle *a* or *b*.

1. swimming pool     a.          b.

2. bookshelf     a.          b.

3. bedroom     a.          b.

4. shopping mall     a.          b.

5. driveway     a.          b.

6. post office     a.          b.

7. grandson     a.          b.

8. mailbox     a.          b.

9. living room     a.          b.

10. fireplace     a.          b.

swimming pool

fireplace

**B.** Write six sentences with the compound nouns in Activity A. Then read your sentences to a partner.

1. _____

2. _____

3. _____

4. _____

5. _____

6. _____

iQ ONLINE **C.** Go online for more practice with stress in compound nouns.

# SPEAKING

**UNIT OBJECTIVE**  At the end of this unit, you are going to design your perfect home and present your design to the class.

## Grammar    *Part 1* Prepositions of location

Prepositions of location answer the question, "Where?"

Use *in* with countries and cities.

The Eiffel Tower is **in Paris**.

Use *on* with the names of streets and roads.

The apartment is **on Oak Street**.

Use *at* with a place in a city or a specific address.

The study group meets **at my house**.      My house is **at 333 Oak Street**.

**A.** Circle the correct preposition.

1. Sam is staying ( in / on / at ) his brother's apartment.

2. Emma lives ( in / on / at ) Shanghai.

3. Hassan's house is ( in / on / at ) Oak Street.

4. The post office is ( in / on / at ) 415 First Street.

5. The bank is ( in / on / at ) Ocean Avenue.

6. The university is ( in / on / at ) Miami.

**B.** Answer the questions with information about you. Use *in*, *on*, and *at* in your answers. Practice the questions and answers with a partner.

1. A: What country do you live in?

   B: _____.

2. A: What city do you live in?

   B: _____.

3. A: What street do you live on?

   B: _____.

4. **A:** What address do you live at?

   **B:** _____

Look at the map and read the paragraph. Notice the bold prepositions of location.

> The bank is **next to** the library. The library is **between** the bank and the gift shop. The gift shop is **across** (the street) **from** the bookstore. The bookstore is **on the corner of** Oak Street and Central Avenue. The parking lot is **behind** the supermarket.

**A.** Look at the map. Complete the sentences with prepositions of location.

1. The library is _____ the bank.

2. The gift shop is _____ Oak Street and Central Avenue.

3. The playground is _____ Jackson Park.

4. The museum is _____ the bookstore and the coffee shop.

5. The coffee shop is _____ the supermarket.

6. Jackson Park is _____ Oak Street and Central Avenue.

7. The bookstore is _____ the museum.

8. The bank is _____ Jackson Park.

**B.** **There is an error in each sentence. Find the errors and correct them.**

1. My apartment building is ~~on~~ *at* 698 Pine Street.

2. The bookstore is in the corner of Central Avenue and Oak Street.

3. The library is between to the bank and the gift shop.

4. The bank is across the street to Jackson Park.

5. The playground is behind of Jackson Park.

6. The museum is next from the coffee shop.

**C.** **Write sentences about places in your city. Use the prepositions of location.**

1. (on the corner of) _____

   _____

2. (across the street from) _____

   _____

3. (behind)_____

4. (between)_____

5. (next to) _____

**D.** **Go online for more practice with prepositions of location.**

**E.** **Go online for the grammar expansion.**

**UNIT OBJECTIVE** ▶▶▶▶

In this assignment, you are going to design your perfect home and present your design to the class. Think about the unit question, "What makes a good home?" Use Listening 1, Listening 2, the unit video, and your work in this unit. Look at the Self-Assessment checklist on page 90.

## CONSIDER THE IDEAS

Listen to the presentation. Check (✓) the ideas that the speakers give.

| **1. What is the inside of the house like?** | |
| --- | --- |
| ☐ four bedrooms | ☐ comfortable chairs and sofas |
| ☐ three bathrooms | ☐ a big television |
| ☐ a big kitchen | ☐ big windows |
| ☐ a big living room | |

| **2. What is the outside of the home like?** | |
| --- | --- |
| ☐ a big backyard | ☐ trees and flowers |
| ☐ a big front yard | ☐ a big driveway |
| ☐ a table with chairs | ☐ a swimming pool |

| **3. What is the neighborhood like?** | |
| --- | --- |
| ☐ near a shopping mall | ☐ near a supermarket |
| ☐ across the street from a park | ☐ quiet |
| ☐ near public transportation | ☐ nice neighbors |

## PREPARE AND SPEAK

**A.** **FIND IDEAS** Work with a group of three. Make a chart like the one above. Talk about the questions in the chart and write down your ideas. During your discussion, name pros and cons of living in different places. Use expressions for giving your opinions, agreeing, and disagreeing.

**Skill Review**   Agreeing and disagreeing

Remember: During your discussion, you can agree and disagree politely using the expressions below. Review the Speaking Skill box in Unit 4 on page 66.

| **Agreeing** | I do too. / Me too. | I don't either. / Me neither. |
| --- | --- | --- |
| **Disagreeing** | Oh, I don't know. | I'm not sure. |

**B.** **ORGANIZE IDEAS** Look at your chart in Activity A. Choose the four most important items in each column. Follow these steps.

1. Draw a map of your perfect home.
   - Draw the rooms inside the house.
   - Draw the outside of the house.
   - Show some of the neighborhood.

2. Each person chooses one part of the home to describe.

3. Practice your presentation.

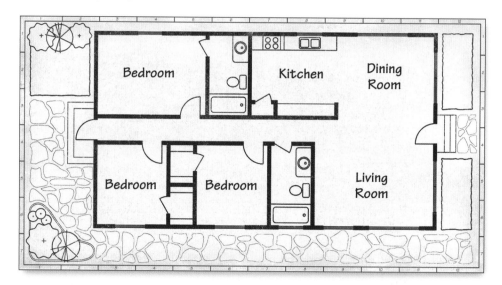

**C.** **SPEAK** Put your home drawing on the wall. Take turns presenting information about your home. Look at the Self-Assessment checklist below before you begin.

 Go online for your alternate Unit Assignment.

## CHECK AND REFLECT

**A.** **CHECK** Think about the Unit Assignment as you complete the Self-Assessment checklist.

| SELF-ASSESSMENT | | |
|---|---|---|
| Yes | No | |
| ☐ | ☐ | My information was clear. |
| ☐ | ☐ | I used vocabulary from this unit. |
| ☐ | ☐ | I used prepositions of location correctly. |
| ☐ | ☐ | I listened for the opinions of my group members. |
| ☐ | ☐ | I agreed and disagreed with opinions appropriately. |

**B.** **REFLECT** Go to the Online Discussion Board to discuss these questions.

1. What is something new you learned in this unit?

2. Think about the Unit Question—What makes a good home? Is your answer different now than when you started this unit? If yes, how is it different? Why?

# TRACK YOUR SUCCESS

**Circle the words and phrases you have learned in this unit.**

| **Nouns** | location **AWL** | **Adjectives** |
|---|---|---|
| backyard | mailbox | affordable |
| bathroom 🔑 | police officer | comfortable 🔑 |
| bathtub | post office | noisy 🔑 |
| bedroom 🔑 | public transportation | private 🔑 |
| bookshelf | rent 🔑 | **Prepositions** |
| condition 🔑 | roommate | across from 🔑 |
| demand 🔑 | shopping mall | at 🔑 |
| driveway | shortage | behind 🔑 |
| drugstore | smoke alarm | between 🔑 |
| entertainment 🔑 | streetcar | in 🔑 |
| extended family | swimming pool | near 🔑 |
| fireplace | | next to 🔑 |
| housing | **Verb** | on 🔑 |
| landlord | increase 🔑 | on the corner of |

🔑 Oxford 2000 keywords
**AWL** Academic Word List

**Check (✓) the skills you learned. If you need more work on a skill, refer to the page(s) in parentheses.**

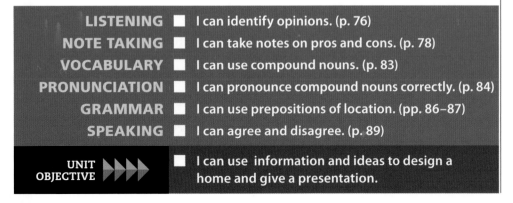

| LISTENING | ☐ I can identify opinions. (p. 76) |
|---|---|
| NOTE TAKING | ☐ I can take notes on pros and cons. (p. 78) |
| VOCABULARY | ☐ I can use compound nouns. (p. 83) |
| PRONUNCIATION | ☐ I can pronounce compound nouns correctly. (p. 84) |
| GRAMMAR | ☐ I can use prepositions of location. (pp. 86–87) |
| SPEAKING | ☐ I can agree and disagree. (p. 89) |
| UNIT OBJECTIVE ▶▶▶▶ | ☐ I can use information and ideas to design a home and give a presentation. |

UNIT 6

Health Sciences

| LISTENING | ▶ | listening for frequency |
| NOTE TAKING | ▶ | taking notes in a chart |
| VOCABULARY | ▶ | adjectives ending in *-ed* |
| GRAMMAR | ▶ | modals *can* and *should* |
| PRONUNCIATION | ▶ | stressing important words |
| SPEAKING | ▶ | asking for repetition |

**UNIT QUESTION**

# What do you do to stay healthy?

**A** Discuss these questions with your classmates.

1. Check (✓) the statements that are true for you. Then compare with a partner. How do you think these things affect your health?

☐ I eat a lot of sweets.　　☐ I watch television every day.

☐ I exercise a lot.　　　　☐ I am on a sports team.

☐ I drink a lot of water.　　☐ I worry a lot.

2. Look at the photo. How does this person stay healthy?

◗ **B** Listen to *The Q Classroom* online. Then answer these questions.

1. What did the students say? Who do you think has the healthiest habits?

2. Which student are you most like? How?

 **C** Go to the Online Discussion Board to discuss the Unit Question with your classmates.

UNIT
OBJECTIVE ▶▶▶▶ Listen to some interviews. Then use information
and ideas to make a health survey and discuss it
with a partner.

## LISTENING 1 | Health Watch

**UNIT OBJECTIVE** ▶▶▶ You are going to listen to an interview about stress. Think about how you stay healthy.

### PREVIEW THE LISTENING

**A.** **VOCABULARY** Here are some words from Listening 1. Read the definitions. Then complete the sentences below.

> **diet** (*noun*) the food that you usually eat
>
> **energy** (*noun*) 🔑 the ability to be active and not become tired
>
> **lonely** (*adjective*) 🔑 sad because you are not with other people
>
> **manage** (*verb*) 🔑 to control something
>
> **reduce** (*verb*) 🔑 to make something smaller
>
> **run-down** (*adjective*) very tired and not healthy, often because you are working too hard
>
> **stress** (*noun*) 🔑 a feeling of being very worried because of problems in your life

🔑 Oxford 2000 keywords

**Vocabulary Skill Review**

In Unit 3, you learned about prefixes and suffixes. Look at the sentences in Activity A. Can you find any words with the prefix *un-*? What do you think the suffix *-ful* means?

1. Ziyad is sad because he feels _____. He doesn't have many friends in his new city.

2. Kate works 60 hours a week. She wants to _____ her time at work to 40 hours a week.

3. Lin is feeling a lot of _____ right now. She has three exams this week!

4. I don't have any _____. I feel tired all the time.

5. Sam has an unhealthy _____. He has pizza and soda for lunch every day. He hardly ever eats vegetables.

**pizza and soda**

6. Anna doesn't _____ her schedule very well. She's always late and she often forgets to do her homework.

7. Hiroshi is working two jobs and taking four classes. He looks really _____.

**B.** Go online for more practice with the vocabulary.

**C.** **PREVIEW** You are going to listen to an interview with Dr. Michael Smith about stress. When do people feel stress? Check (✓) your answers and add one more idea.

**People can feel stress when...**

- ☐ they have money problems.
- ☐ they want good grades.
- ☐ they work long hours.
- ☐ they have healthy diets.
- ☐ they are lonely.
- ☐ _____

# WORK WITH THE LISTENING

**A.** Listen to the interview. Circle the correct answers.

1. What is the main topic of this interview?
   - a. exercise
   - b. stress
   - c. money
   - d. students

2. What is the **big** cause of stress these days?
   - a. People are too busy.
   - b. People don't have jobs.
   - c. People eat bad food.
   - d. People are lonely.

3. What are two causes of stress for many students?
   - a. money and health
   - b. diet and no exercise
   - c. work and grades
   - d. grades and children

**4.** What is "a great way to reduce stress"?

   a. getting a job                b. having children

   c. exercising every day       d. laughing

**B.** Listen to the interview. What ideas and topics does the interview mention? Circle the ideas and topics.

| | | | | |
|---|---|---|---|---|
| vacations | money | sickness | vegetables | coffee |
| (work) | rent | headaches | exercise | friends |
| children | grades | sleep | food | medicine |

**C.** Read the sentences in the chart. Then listen again. Check (✓) the correct column for each sentence.

**Tip for Success**

The verb *cause* means "to make something happen." Here, you see the noun form of *cause*. It means "a thing that makes something happen."

| | Causes of stress | Symptoms of stress | Ways to reduce stress |
|---|---|---|---|
| **1.** People feel run-down. | ☐ | ☑ | ☐ |
| **2.** They exercise. | ☐ | ☐ | ☐ |
| **3.** They worry about money. | ☐ | ☐ | ☐ |
| **4.** They have a good diet. | ☐ | ☐ | ☐ |
| **5.** They're very busy. | ☐ | ☐ | ☐ |
| **6.** They don't have energy. | ☐ | ☐ | ☐ |
| **7.** They feel lonely. | ☐ | ☐ | ☐ |
| **8.** They have social time. | ☐ | ☐ | ☐ |
| **9.** They gain weight. | ☐ | ☐ | ☐ |
| **10.** They worry about grades. | ☐ | ☐ | ☐ |

**D.** Read the sentences. Write *T* (true) or *F* (false) for each statement. Then correct each false statement.

_____ **1.** People are too busy because they feel stress.

_____

_____ **2.** Many people have children and work full time.

_____

_____ **3.** Dr. Smith thinks that money is sometimes a cause of stress.

_____

_____ 4. Students don't have many problems with stress.

_____

_____ 5. Some people have stress because of worrying.

_____

_____ 6. Stress sometimes makes people sick.

_____

_____ 7. Exercise does not reduce stress.

_____

_____ 8. Laughter helps to reduce stress.

_____

 **E.** Go online to listen to *Exercise for Your Health* and check your comprehension.

 ## SAY WHAT YOU THINK

**When do you feel stress? Add one idea to the chart. Check (✓) your answers. Then discuss your answers with a partner.**

|  | A lot of stress | A little stress | Not any stress |
|---|---|---|---|
| With my family | ☐ | ☐ | ☐ |
| At school | ☐ | ☐ | ☐ |
| With my neighbors | ☐ | ☐ | ☐ |
| At work | ☐ | ☐ | ☐ |
| With my friends | ☐ | ☐ | ☐ |
| _____ | ☐ | ☐ | ☐ |

**Frequency** means "How often?" When you listen, try to hear these frequency adverbs and expressions.

| Adverbs of frequency | always, usually, often, sometimes, hardly ever, never |
|---|---|
| Expressions with *every* | **every** day, **every** week, **every** year |
| Other expressions | **once a** week, **twice a** month, three **times a** year<br>eight **hours a** day, four **hours a** week |

A: Do you **always** exercise at the gym?
B: No, **sometimes** I jog in the park.
A: How often do you exercise?
B: **Three times a week.**

**A.** Listen to eight parts of a conversation. Circle the words and expressions you hear. (Three items have two answers.)

1. always          sometimes          every week

2. never           every day          once a week

3. twice a week    never              sometimes

4. six days a week twice a week       every day

5. always          sometimes          three times a week

6. once a week     usually            twice a week

7. usually         once a day         always

8. every week      once a day         three times a week

**B.** Read the questions. Listen to the whole conversation. Circle the correct answers.

1. How many days a week does John work?
   a. five          b. six          c. seven

2. How often does John exercise?
   a. every day          b. twice a week          c. never

3. How often does Anna go to the gym?
   a. three days a week          b. six days a week          c. every day

4. How often does Anna go running?
   a. twice a week          b. three times a week          c. once a week

5. How often does John drink coffee with his meals?
   a. sometimes          b. always          c. usually

**C.** Ask and answer these questions with a partner. Write your partner's answers.

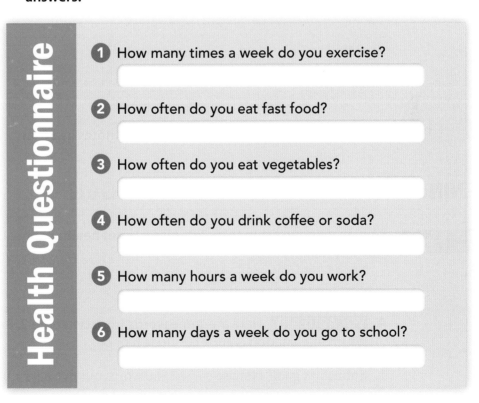

**Health Questionnaire**

1 How many times a week do you exercise?

2 How often do you eat fast food?

3 How often do you eat vegetables?

4 How often do you drink coffee or soda?

5 How many hours a week do you work?

6 How many days a week do you go to school?

 **D.** Go online for more practice with listening for frequency.

In Unit 4 on page 54, you learned about using a T-chart. When you listen, sometimes you hear a lot of information. For example, two or three people talk about their lives. For complicated information, a T-chart is too simple. Use a bigger chart. Look at the chart below. The more complicated information about each person is clearly organized.

| Name | Healthy Habits | Unhealthy Habits |
|------|----------------|------------------|
| Jin | eats a lot of vegetables | doesn't work out at all |
| Tania | runs every day | eats a lot of junk food |

**A.** Listen to three students talk about their healthy and unhealthy habits. Then complete the chart with the missing information.

| Name | Healthy Habits | Unhealthy Habits |
|------|----------------|------------------|
| Emma | works out five days a week | |
| Amal | | |
| John | | |

 **B.** Go online for more practice with taking notes in a chart.

## LISTENING 2 | How Often Do You Work Out?

 **UNIT OBJECTIVE** You are going to listen to an interview about health habits. Think about how you stay healthy.

## PREVIEW THE LISTENING

**A. VOCABULARY** Here are some words from Listening 2. Read the sentences. Which explanation is correct? Circle *a* or *b*.

1. Emma has good exercise <u>habits</u>. She works out five days a week.
   a. Emma exercises very often.
   b. Emma has nice exercise clothes.

I watch what I eat.

2. John likes to <u>stay in shape</u>. He goes to the gym almost every day.
   a. John spends a lot of time indoors.
   b. John takes care of his body and health.

3. Fatima wants to <u>prepare</u> dinner for us. She is an excellent cook.
   a. Fatima wants to go out for dinner.
   b. Fatima wants to make dinner.

4. Miteb goes to the gym <u>regularly</u>. He works out every evening after work.
   a. Miteb exercises very often.
   b. Miteb doesn't exercise every week.

5. Nour goes running <u>at least</u> three times a week. If he has time, he runs more.
   a. Nour sometimes runs only twice a week.
   b. Nour sometimes runs four times a week.

6. I <u>watch what I eat</u>. For example, I don't eat food with a lot of fat or sugar.
   a. The speaker chooses her food carefully.
   b. The speaker chooses cheap and convenient food.

7. Amal sells houses <u>for a living</u>. She works five days a week.
   a. Amal sells houses as a job.
   b. Amal's house is too big. She wants to sell it.

8. I started exercising last month, and I want to <u>keep it up</u>. I feel a lot better.
   a. The speaker wants to continue exercising this month.
   b. The speaker wants to stop exercising this month.

I started exercising.

**B.** Go online for more practice with the vocabulary.

**C.** PREVIEW You are going to listen to an interview with three people at a gym about their health habits.

What do people with good health habits do? What do people with bad health habits do? Write your ideas in the chart. Then compare your ideas with a partner.

| People with good health habits... | People with bad health habits... |
|---|---|
| watch what they eat | eat junk food |

**Critical Thinking** Tip

In Activity C, you **compare** the actions of people with good health habits and people with bad health habits. Comparing things is a way to understand them more deeply.

# WORK WITH THE LISTENING

**A.** Listen to the interviews with Matt, Kate, and Rob. Match each person with the correct description.

1. Matt ____     a. is a lawyer.

2. Kate ____     b. is a manager at a store.

3. Rob ____      c. is a history teacher.

**B.** Look at the chart. Then listen again. Check (✓) the correct information for each person. (You will check more than one column.)

| | Sleeps at least eight hours a night | Exercises at least three times a week | Doesn't work too much | Eats healthy food |
|---|---|---|---|---|
| **1.** Matt | ☐ | ✓ | ☐ | ☐ |
| **2.** Kate | ☐ | ☐ | ☐ | ☐ |
| **3.** Rob | ☐ | ☐ | ☐ | ☐ |

**C.** Complete the chart. Compare your answers with a partner.

| Name | Healthy habits | Unhealthy habits |
|---|---|---|
| Matt | | |
| Kate | | |
| Rob | | |

**D.** Use your notes from Activity C to answer the questions below. Check (✓) the correct name. Then compare your answers with a partner.

| | Kate | Matt | Rob |
|---|---|---|---|
| 1. Who is a vegetarian? | ☐ | ☐ | ☐ |
| 2. Who works out for two hours every day? | ☐ | ☐ | ☐ |
| 3. Who eats junk food? | ☐ | ☐ | ☐ |
| 4. Who works seven days a week? | ☐ | ☐ | ☐ |
| 5. Who sleeps ten hours a night? | ☐ | ☐ | ☐ |
| 6. Who hates exercising? | ☐ | ☐ | ☐ |
| 7. Who reads and walks in the park to relax? | ☐ | ☐ | ☐ |
| 8. Who works 12 to 13 hours a day? | ☐ | ☐ | ☐ |
| 9. Who sleeps only five hours a night? | ☐ | ☐ | ☐ |

**E.** Read the sentences. Write *T* (true) or *F* (false) for each statement. Then correct each false statement to make it true.

_____ 1. Matt hardly ever exercises.

_____ 2. Kate works out three days a week or more.

_____ 3. Rob chooses his food carefully.

____ **4.** Matt works only five hours a day.

____ **5.** Rob teaches business management.

____ **6.** Kate often gets eight hours of sleep.

____ **7.** Kate likes walking in the park and reading.

____ **8.** Rob likes exercising.

## SAY WHAT YOU THINK

**A.** Make true statements about your health habits. Circle your answers and add your own idea. Then check (✓) your good habits.

**Good Habits**

**1.** I **exercise / don't exercise** regularly. ☐

**2.** I **eat / don't eat** fresh fruits and vegetables. ☐

**3.** I **eat / don't eat** a lot of junk food. ☐

**4.** I **sleep / don't sleep** at least eight hours a night. ☐

**5.** I **work / don't work** too much. ☐

**6.** I **watch / don't watch** what I eat. ☐

**7.** I **do / don't do** relaxing activities. ☐

**8.** Your idea: _____ ☐

**B.** Before you watch the video, discuss these questions with a group.

**1.** Do you have a healthy diet? Why or why not?

**2.** What healthy foods do you eat? What unhealthy foods do you eat?

**3.** Do you take vitamins? Why or why not?

**C.** Go online to watch a video about vitamins. Then check your comprehension.

VIDEO VOCABULARY

**manufacturer** (*n.*) a person or a company that makes something
**produce** (*v.*) to make or grow something
**supplement** (*n.*) something that you add; an addition

**D.** Think about the unit video, Listening 1, and Listening 2 as you discuss these questions.

1. What are your healthy habits?

2. What are your unhealthy habits?

3. How well do you manage stress?

## Building Vocabulary | Adjectives ending in *-ed*

**Tip for Success**

Adjectives ending in *-ed* look like past tense verbs. A verb usually comes after a noun or subject pronoun. (*Anna **surprised** us.*) An adjective usually comes after a form of *be*. (*Anna is **surprised**.*)

Many adjectives end with *-ed*. These adjectives come from verbs. They usually describe a feeling or an emotion.

| Verbs | John <u>worries</u> a lot. | Anna likes to <u>relax</u> at the park. |
| --- | --- | --- |
| Adjectives | John is **worried**. | Anna is **relaxed**. |

Here are some other adjectives ending with *-ed*.

bored    confused    excited    interested    relaxed    surprised    tired

**A.** Read the sentences. Complete each sentence with the adjective form of the word in bold.

1. Mary **worries** about school. She is always _____.

2. Soccer games **excite** James. He is _____ to play soccer today.

3. Running doesn't **interest** me. I'm not _____ in running.

4. Sam **relaxes** on the weekends. On Saturdays, he is usually

_____.

5. These questions **confuse** me. I'm _____.

**B.** Complete each conversation with a word from the box. Then practice the conversations with a partner. You won't use all of the words.

| bored   excited   interested   relaxed   surprised   tired   worried |

1. A: What's wrong?

   B: Oh, I'm a little _____. I stayed awake really late

   last night.

2. A: I'm _____. Let's do something fun.

   B: Do you want to play tennis?

3. A: Guess what! My brother wants to go to the gym with us tomorrow!

   B: Wow, I'm _____! He hates exercising!

4. A: I'm _____ about the final exam. This class is really

   difficult for me.

   B: I plan to study with Isabel and Emma tonight. You can join us. Are

   you _____?

   A: Yes, I am! Thanks!

 **C.** Go online for more practice with adjectives ending in *-ed*.

# SPEAKING

**UNIT OBJECTIVE** ▶▶▶▶ At the end of this unit, you are going to make a health survey and discuss it with a partner.

## Grammar   Modals *can* and *should*

1. A modal comes before a base form verb. Modals can be affirmative or negative.*

   ☐   I **should eat** more fruit.       I **can't sleep** some nights.
        modal base verb             modal base verb

   Don't put an **-s** at the end of the verb.

   ☐   ✓ Correct: He **can play** tennis well.    ✗ Incorrect: He **can plays** tennis well.

2. Use **can / can't** to talk about possibility or ability.

   ☐   Stress **can make** people gain weight.    Rob **can't swim**.

3. Use **should / shouldn't** to give advice.

   ☐   You **should exercise** every day.       You **shouldn't worry** all the time.

   *The full forms of *shouldn't* and *can't* are *should not* and *cannot*.

He works too much.

**A.** Complete the conversation with *can*, *can't*, *should*, and *shouldn't*. Then practice with a partner.

**Hyo:** I'm worried about Martin. He looks really tired. He works too much.

**Jamal:** I know. He _____ work so much.
                    1

**Hyo:** You're right. He _____ sleep more, too. He sleeps about
                               2
four hours a night! And he doesn't exercise.

**Jamal:** He _____ come to the gym with me. There's a great
                     3
swimming pool there.

**Hyo:** Well, he _____ swim, but he wants to learn.
                        4
Does your gym have swimming lessons?

**Jamal:** Yes, it does. He _____ take lessons in the evenings or
                             5
on the weekends.

**Hyo:** Oh, good. You _____ call him and tell him that.
            6

I _____ come, too. I need to learn how to swim.
        7

**Jamal:** Yes, that's a great idea!

**B.** Write three sentences about stress in your life and your bad habits. (Look at the information you wrote in the *Say What You Think* Activities on pages 104 and 105.)

1. _____

2. _____

3. _____

**C.** Take turns reading your sentences with a partner. Give your partner advice. Use *should* and *shouldn't*.

*A: I feel a lot of stress because I worry about grades.*
*B: Hmm. You should…*

**iQ** ONLINE **D.** Go online for more practice with the modals *can* and *should*.

**E.** Go online for the grammar expansion.

---

**Pronunciation** | **Stressing important words**

Speakers sometimes stress important words, like nouns, verbs, and adverbs of frequency. Speakers use stress to:

- **answer a question.** Speakers stress the words with the answer to the question.

- **correct mistakes.** Speakers stress the word they are correcting.

| Answering a question | Correcting a mistake |
|---|---|
| **A:** How often do you exercise? | **A:** I can swim. |
| **B:** I exercise **every day**. | **B:** You can't swim? |
| | **A:** No, I **can** swim. |

**A.** Underline the stressed words in the conversation. Listen to check your answers. Then practice the conversations with a partner.

1. **A:** Are you worried? **B:** No, I'm feeling <u>relaxed</u>.

2. **A:** Do you go to the gym on Fridays? **B:** No, I go on Saturdays.

3. **A:** Should I drive downtown? **B:** No, you should walk!

4. **A:** Do you exercise every day? **B:** No, I only exercise on the weekends.

5. **A:** I can't play tennis.

   **B:** You can play tennis? Let's go!

   **A:** No, I can't play tennis.

**fast food**

**B.** Write answers to the questions. Then circle the stressed words in your answers.

1. How often do you exercise?

2. How much stress do you have in your life?

3. What do you worry about?

4. How often do you eat fast food?

**C.** Work with a partner. Ask and answer the questions in Activity B together.

**D.** Go online for more practice with stressing important words.

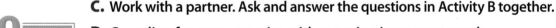

| Speaking Skill | Asking for repetition |

Use these expressions to ask for repetition when you don't understand something.

| Excuse me? | Sorry. What did you say? |
|---|---|
| **A:** Do you worry about money? | **A:** There's a new health-food restaurant downtown. |
| **B:** Excuse me? | **B:** Sorry. What did you say? |
| **A:** Do you sometimes worry about money? | **A:** There's a new restaurant downtown. They have health food. |
| **B:** No, not really. | **B:** Oh, that sounds good! |

We often use the expression *I'm sorry. Could you repeat that?* when we have asked for information but don't understand the answer.

We often ask for repetition of **numbers** because many numbers have similar sounds.

> **I'm sorry. Could you repeat that?**
>
> **A:** How much does the health club cost?
> **B:** It's $30 a month.
> **A:** I'm sorry. Could you repeat that?
> **B:** Sure. It's $30 every month.

**A. Listen to Martin talk to his doctor. Answer the questions.**

1. What are Martin's symptoms?
   a. He is always worried and unhappy.
   b. He is always tired and often sick.

2. How many hours does he work every week?
   a. 15 or 16                     b. 50 or 60

3. How often does Martin take vacations?
   a. every month                  b. never

4. What does he sometimes do for exercise?
   a. He swims.                    b. He runs.

**B. Work with a partner. Ask and answer these questions about health. Ask for repetition.**

1. What do you worry about?

2. How often do you feel tired?

3. How many hours do you work or study?

4. What should you do more of?

5. What are five things that you can do to stay healthy?

 **C. Go online for more practice with asking for repetition.**

In this assignment, you are going to make a health survey. Then you are going to discuss the survey with a partner. Think about the Unit Question, "What do you do to stay healthy?" Use Listening 1, Listening 2, the unit video, and your work in this unit. Look at the Self-Assessment checklist on page 112.

## CONSIDER THE IDEAS

Listen to some students discuss their survey. Check (✓) the questions that you hear.

☐ 1. How many hours do you work every week?
☐ 2. How many hours do you sleep every night?
☐ 3. How often do you exercise?
☐ 4. What do you do with your friends?
☐ 5. What do you do to relax?

## PREPARE AND SPEAK

**A. FIND IDEAS** Work with a partner. Write six questions about health habits. Include questions about diet, sleep, and work.

1. _____
2. _____
3. _____
4. _____
5. _____
6. _____

**B. ORGANIZE IDEAS** With your partner, look at your health questions from Activity A. Choose the three best questions and add them below and on page 112.

Question 1: _____

Student 1: _____

Student 2: _____

Student 3: _____

**Question 2:** _____

Student 1: _____

Student 2: _____

Student 3: _____

**Question 3:** _____

Student 1: _____

Student 2: _____

Student 3: _____

**C.** **SPEAK** Follow these steps. Look at the Self-Assessment checklist below before you begin.

1. Work individually. Ask three students your questions. Write their answers above. You and your partner should talk to different people.

2. Share your survey answers with your partner. Discuss your survey results.

 Go online for your alternate Unit Assignment.

## CHECK AND REFLECT

**A.** **CHECK** Think about the Unit Assignment as you complete the Self-Assessment checklist.

| SELF-ASSESSMENT | | |
|---|---|---|
| Yes | No | |
| ☐ | ☐ | My information was clear. |
| ☐ | ☐ | I used vocabulary from this unit. |
| ☐ | ☐ | I used a chart to take notes. |
| ☐ | ☐ | I used the modals *can*, *can't*, *should*, and *shouldn't* correctly. |
| ☐ | ☐ | I used adjectives ending with *-ed* correctly. |
| ☐ | ☐ | I listened for frequency expressions. |

 **B.** **REFLECT** Go to the Online Discussion Board to discuss these questions.

1. What is something new you learned in this unit?

2. Think about the Unit Question—What do you do to stay healthy? Is your answer different now than when you started this unit? If yes, how is it different? Why?

# TRACK YOUR SUCCESS

**Circle the words and phrases you have learned in this unit.**

**Nouns**
cause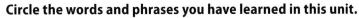
diet
energy AWL
habit
stress AWL

**Verbs**
keep (something) up
manage
prepare
reduce

**Adjectives**
bored
confused
excited
interested
lonely
relaxed AWL
run-down
surprised
tired
worried

**Adverbs**
at least
regularly

**Phrases**
for a living
stay in shape
watch what (I) eat

**Modals**
can
should

Oxford 2000 keywords
AWL Academic Word List

**Check (✓) the skills you learned. If you need more work on a skill, refer to the page(s) in parentheses.**

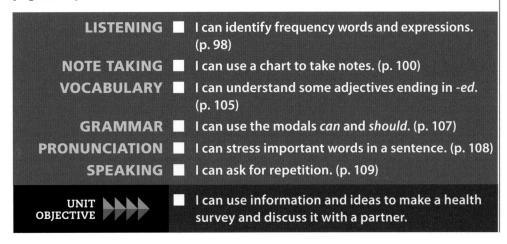

| | |
|---|---|
| **LISTENING** ■ | I can identify frequency words and expressions. (p. 98) |
| **NOTE TAKING** ■ | I can use a chart to take notes. (p. 100) |
| **VOCABULARY** ■ | I can understand some adjectives ending in -*ed*. (p. 105) |
| **GRAMMAR** ■ | I can use the modals *can* and *should*. (p. 107) |
| **PRONUNCIATION** ■ | I can stress important words in a sentence. (p. 108) |
| **SPEAKING** ■ | I can ask for repetition. (p. 109) |
| **UNIT OBJECTIVE** ▶▶▶▶ ■ | I can use information and ideas to make a health survey and discuss it with a partner. |

NOTE TAKING ▶ taking notes in an informal outline
LISTENING ▶ review: listening for frequency
VOCABULARY ▶ using the dictionary: word families
GRAMMAR ▶ past of *be*; simple past affirmative statements
PRONUNCIATION ▶ *-ed* endings
SPEAKING ▶ using open questions

**UNIT QUESTION**

# What makes a city special?

**A** Discuss these questions with your classmates.

1. What are three special places in your city or town?

2. What activities can you do in your city or town?

3. What is your favorite city? Why?

4. Look at the photo. What do you see? What is special about this city? Why do people come here?

**B** Listen to *The Q Classroom* online. Then answer these questions.

1. What did the students say makes a city special?

2. Which things that you listed in Activity A did the students mention?

3. Which do you like better, big cities or small towns?

 **C** Go to the Online Discussion Board to discuss the Unit Question with your classmates.

UNIT
OBJECTIVE

Listen to a radio program and a speech. Use information
and ideas to give a presentation about a special city.

It's important to take organized notes that show you how ideas are related. An **informal outline** is an easy way to see how one idea is related to another idea. It's also easy to find information in your notes when you study.

Read this sample from a radio show.

> David:  Thanks for joining us on *Travel Talk*, Amy. What city did you visit?
>
> Amy:    I'm happy to be here, David. I visited Seoul, South Korea, last month. It's a beautiful city with interesting architecture. There are big skyscrapers downtown. And there are some traditional wooden houses, too.

Look at the page of notes. Notice the note-taker used an informal outline. The bigger, more important ideas are close to the the left margin of the paper. Details about each big idea are below and to the right.

> *City*
> > *Seoul*
> *Architecture*
> > *skyscrapers*
> > *some traditional buildings*

**A.** Read the rest of the conversation. Take informal notes on the food and activities in Seoul.

> David:  Did you like the food?
>
> Amy:    The food was great. It was spicy and delicious. I really liked the noodles and the beef.
>
> David:  What kinds of things did you do?
>
> Amy:    Well, I did a lot of shopping. Seoul has some great department stores. There are also some fun outdoor markets.
>
> David:  That sounds like fun. What else did you do?
>
> Amy:    I went hiking one day in the mountains.

 **B.** Go online for more practice with taking notes in an informal outline.

# LISTENING

## LISTENING 1 | Travel Talk

**UNIT OBJECTIVE** ▶▶▶

You are going to listen to a radio program about three special cities. Think about what makes a city special.

## PREVIEW THE LISTENING

**A. VOCABULARY** Here are some words from Listening 1. Read the sentences. Which explanation is correct? Circle *a* or *b*.

1. The climate of Tunisia includes hot and dry summers.
   a. The weather is hot and dry in Tunisia in the summer.
   b. The beaches of Tunisia are hot and dry in the summer.

2. The average tourist stays at this hotel for one week, but Anna really likes it here. She is staying two weeks.
   a. Anna is like most tourists at the hotel.
   b. Anna is not like most tourists at the hotel.

Kyoto

3. Many tourists visit Kyoto because it is a center for Japanese culture. They go to Kyoto to have good Japanese food, visit museums, and see beautiful old buildings.
   a. You can learn a lot about Japanese customs and culture in Kyoto.
   b. You can do a lot of shopping in Kyoto.

4. You can walk through the gardens at the park. You can also go to lectures there. You can listen to someone give a talk about a subject you are interested in.
   a. A lecture is a kind of talk.
   b. A garden is a kind of talk.

5. Mary recently visited Shanghai. She was there last month.
   a. Mary visited Shanghai a short time ago.
   b. Mary visited Shanghai a long time ago.

the Roman Forum

6. Rome has several historic buildings. For example, the famous Forum is in Rome. It is about 2,000 years old.
   a. Rome has many important new buildings.
   b. Rome has many important old buildings.

7. Rio de Janeiro has many <u>skyscrapers</u>. One of them is Ventura Corporate Towers. It has 38 floors. Some skyscrapers have more than 40 floors.

   a. There are a lot of big offices in Rio.

   b. There are a lot of tall buildings in Rio.

 **B.** Go online for more practice with the vocabulary.

**C.** **PREVIEW** You are going to listen to a radio program about three special cities. Look at the pictures. Match each description with the correct picture. Write the letters.

1. \_\_\_\_        2. \_\_\_\_        3. \_\_\_\_

a. Ubud is on an island in Bali, in Indonesia.

b. Bruges is a historic city in Belgium. It has canals and colorful houses.

c. New York City is a busy city in the United States.

## WORK WITH THE LISTENING

 **A.** Listen to the radio program. The interviewer talks to three people. Match each person with the correct city.

1. David \_\_\_\_        a. Bruges

2. Amanda \_\_\_\_       b. Ubud

3. Sam \_\_\_\_         c. New York City

4. Mika \_\_\_\_         d. does not name a city

Amanda:

City: _____

Architecture

_____

Food

    delicious

Activities

_____

Other information

    on Bali in Indonesia, warm climate, cool and
    comfortable forests, center for culture

Sam:

City: _____

Architecture

_____

Food

_____

Activities

    museums

Mika:

City: _____

Architecture

_____

Food

_____

Activities

    shopping, eating at restaurants and cafés

Other information

    big, modern, busy, over 8 million people

**C.** Look at the outline in Activity B on page 119. Check (✓) the topics that each speaker talks about.

| | climate | architecture | food | shopping | museums | lectures | walks |
|---|---|---|---|---|---|---|---|
| Amanda | | | | | | | |
| Sam | | | | | | | |
| Mika | | | | | | | |

**D.** Read the descriptions of the people. Match each person with the best vacation city. Use the information in your notes in Activity B.

| a. Ubud | b. Bruges | c. New York |
|---|---|---|

____ 1. Eric likes modern cities. He loves to go to museums. He also loves to go shopping and eat different kinds of food.

____ 2. Theresa loves to go to places with beautiful, warm weather.

____ 3. Jonas likes European cities. He is interested in European history.

____ 4. (describe yourself) _____

_____

iQ ONLINE **E.** Go online to listen to *Come to Istanbul!* and check your comprehension.

**Skill Review** | **Listening for frequency**

Remember: Frequency means "How often?" When you listen, try to hear frequency adverbs and expressions like *usually* and *every night*. Review the Listening Skill box in Unit 6 on page 98.

**F.** Read the sentences. Then listen to the radio program again. Circle the answer to complete each statement.

1. The average temperature in Bali is ___.
   a. cool          b. very warm          c. very hot

2. The speaker enjoyed going to lectures and taking walks ___.
   a. every evening    b. every weekend    c. every week

3. According to the speaker, Bruges has ___.
   a. amazing architecture      b. a big shopping mall      c. skyscrapers

4. The speaker thinks Bruges ___ in the world.
   a. is the best place    b. has the best chocolate    c. has the best food

5. The speaker visited New York ___.
   a. last week          b. last month          c. last year

6. One of the speaker's favorite things about New York is ___.
   a. the people          b. the shopping          c. the museums

**G.** Go online for more practice with listening for frequency.

## SAY WHAT YOU THINK

**A.** Work with a partner. Choose a city that you both know. Complete the chart individually.

| City: _____ | Not good | OK | Good |
|---|---|---|---|
| 1. culture | ☐ | ☐ | ☐ |
| 2. architecture | ☐ | ☐ | ☐ |
| 3. weather | ☐ | ☐ | ☐ |
| 4. shopping | ☐ | ☐ | ☐ |
| 5. food | ☐ | ☐ | ☐ |

**B.** Discuss your chart with your partner. Give reasons for your answers.

*A: I think the culture in Tokyo is good.*
*B: I agree. You can go to a lot of museums there.*

# LISTENING 2 | Making Positive Changes

 You are going to listen to a speech about a town. Think about what makes a city special.

## PREVIEW THE LISTENING

**A.** **VOCABULARY** Here are some words from Listening 2. Read the sentences. Then write each <u>underlined</u> word next to the correct definition.

1. I'm not a <u>resident</u> of this city, so I can't borrow books from this library. I can only borrow books from my city's library.

2. The City leaders want to <u>improve</u> public transportation. They plan to buy twenty buses and ten trains this year.

3. The Eiffel Tower in Paris is my favorite <u>monument</u>. I also like the Great Wall of China.

4. This city has so many interesting <u>sights</u>. Let's go to the Natural History Museum this afternoon and the night market this evening.

5. Go to the top of the Empire State Building at night. The <u>view</u> of the city is beautiful.

6. The City leaders want more nature in the park. They asked landscapers to <u>create</u> new gardens.

7. Flights to London are really cheap right now. Let's buy tickets. It's a great <u>opportunity</u>!

8. The park has a <u>variety</u> of activities. We can hike, play basketball, or ride bikes.

a. _____ (*noun*) interesting places in a city or town—tourists like to visit them

b. _____ (*verb*) to make something better

c. _____ (*noun*) all the things you can see from a place

d. _____ (*noun*) a large structure or building—it helps people remember a person or event from the past

e. _____ (*noun*) a lot of different things

f. _____ (*verb*) to make something

g. _____ (*noun*) a person—he or she lives in a city, neighborhood, or building

h. _____ (*noun*) a chance to do something

**B.** Go online for more practice with the vocabulary.

**C.** **PREVIEW** You are going to hear the mayor of Seacliff give a speech about changes in the town during the past year. Look at the photo of a town meeting. Circle the correct words in the sentences.

1. These people are ( visitors / residents ).

2. They are ( at city hall / in a classroom ).

## WORK WITH THE LISTENING

**A.** Listen to the speech. Check (✓) the correct problem and solution for each place. (You will not check all the items.)

| Problems | Parks and beaches | Historic buildings and monuments | Downtown area |
|---|---|---|---|
| 1. They were dirty. | ✓ | ☐ | ☐ |
| 2. They were not safe. | ☐ | ☐ | ☐ |
| 3. They were in bad condition. | ☐ | ☐ | ☐ |
| 4. The shops and restaurants were old. | ☐ | ☐ | ☐ |
| 5. Business was bad. | ☐ | ☐ | ☐ |
| **Solutions** | | | |
| 6. Volunteers cleaned the areas. | ☐ | ☐ | ☐ |
| 7. The city hired more police. | ☐ | ☐ | ☐ |
| 8. Residents gave the city money. | ☐ | ☐ | ☐ |
| 9. The city made repairs and improvements. | ☐ | ☐ | ☐ |
| 10. New shops and restaurants opened. | ☐ | ☐ | ☐ |

**B. Read the sentences. Then listen again. Circle the correct words to complete the sentences.**

1. Seacliff is a ( busy / quiet ) city.

2. Many years ago, ( a lot of tourists / no tourists ) visited Seacliff.

3. The city started having problems because of ( money / a bad mayor ).

4. One historic building in the city is ( the hospital / city hall ).

5. There is a monument to ( the first mayor / the first doctor ) of Seacliff.

6. A lot of the downtown shops closed ( last year / a few years ago ).

7. Seacliff has a new ( college / hotel ).

8. There are more ( residents / jobs ) in Seacliff now.

**Critical Thinking** **Tip**

In Activity C, you **infer** or **make inferences**. This means you make guesses based on information that you hear.

**C. What can you infer from these statements from Listening 2? Circle the correct answers. Some items have more than one answer.**

1. "Our beaches and parks were very dirty."
   a. Seacliff is next to the ocean.
   b. Seacliff is in the mountains.
   c. Seacliff has more than one park.
   d. Seacliff has a lot of visitors.

2. "We have several historic buildings and monuments in Seacliff."
   a. Seacliff is a small town.
   b. Seacliff is a big city.
   c. Seacliff is an old town.
   d. Seacliff is a new town.

3. "We improved the downtown area. . . .Tourists started coming and that created a lot of jobs for our residents."
   a. A lot of the people in Seacliff didn't have jobs last year.
   b. The people in Seacliff don't have jobs now.
   c. People don't like to go downtown because it's crowded.
   d. There were not a lot of jobs downtown last year.

# SAY WHAT YOU THINK

**A.** Discuss these questions in a group.

1. Do you think Seacliff is a nice place to visit? Why or why not?

2. Is Seacliff a nice place to live? Why or why not?

**B.** Go online to watch the video about Dubai. Then check your comprehension.

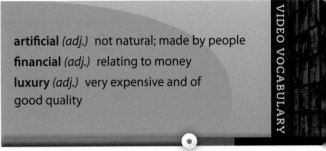

**VIDEO VOCABULARY**

**artificial** *(adj.)* not natural; made by people

**financial** *(adj.)* relating to money

**luxury** *(adj.)* very expensive and of good quality

**C.** Think about video, Listening 1, and Listening 2 as you look at the survey. What does a city need to be special? Check (✓) five things. Number them from 1 (most important) to 5 (least important). Then discuss your answers with a partner.

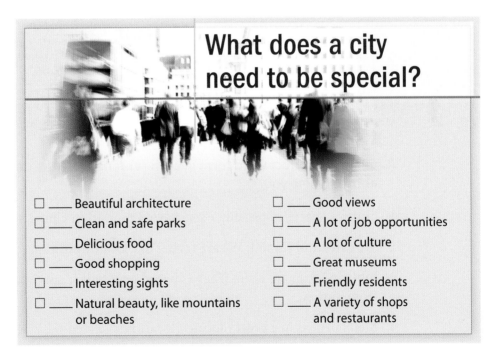

# What does a city need to be special?

- ☐ ___ Beautiful architecture
- ☐ ___ Clean and safe parks
- ☐ ___ Delicious food
- ☐ ___ Good shopping
- ☐ ___ Interesting sights
- ☐ ___ Natural beauty, like mountains or beaches

- ☐ ___ Good views
- ☐ ___ A lot of job opportunities
- ☐ ___ A lot of culture
- ☐ ___ Great museums
- ☐ ___ Friendly residents
- ☐ ___ A variety of shops and restaurants

**Word families** are groups of similar words. Word families can include nouns, verbs, adjectives, and adverbs. For example, look at the related forms of this word:

> **Verb:**       correct
> **Adjective:**  correct
> **Noun:**       correction
> **Adverb:**     correctly

When you look up a word in the dictionary, look for other forms of the word. You can find other word forms in, above, and below the definition. For example, look at the different words forms in, above, and below *locate* and *special*.

**lo·cate** AWL /ˈloʊkeɪt/ *verb* (lo·cates, lo·cat·ing, lo·cat·ed)
to find the exact position of someone or something: *Rescue helicopters are trying to locate the missing sailors.*
► **lo·cat·ed** AWL /ˈloʊkeɪt̬əd/ *adjective*
in a place: *The factory is located near the river.*

**lo·ca·tion** AWL /loʊˈkeɪʃn/ *noun* [count]
a place: *The house is in a quiet location at the top of a hill.*

**spe·cial**¹ 🔑 /ˈspɛʃl/ *adjective*
**1** not usual or ordinary; important for a reason:
**2** for a particular person or thing: *He goes to a special school for deaf children.*

**spe·cial·ize** /ˈspɛʃl·aɪz/ *verb* (spe·cial·iz·es, spe·cial·iz·ing, spe·cial·ized)
**specialize in something** to study or know a lot about one subject, type of product, etc.: *He specialized in criminal law.*

**spe·cial·ly** /ˈspɛʃl·i/ *adverb*
for a particular purpose or reason: *a specially designed chair*

All dictionary entries are from the *Oxford Basic American Dictionary for learners of English.* © Oxford University Press 2011.

**A. Circle the correct word form in each sentence. Use the definitions above to help you.**

1.  This is ( special / specially / specialize ) food from China. It's sweet.

2.  We can't find Khalid. We are trying to ( locate / location / located ) him.

3.  John and Sam are chefs. They ( special / specially / specialize ) in food from Turkey.

4.  Melbourne is in a great ( locate / location / located ). It's next to the ocean and close to beautiful mountains.

5.  My parents cooked me a ( special / specially / specialize ) meal for my graduation.

6. The museum is ( locate / location / **located** ) near city hall.

7. Our lunch is ( special / **specially** / specialize ) prepared. The chef cooked it just for us!

**B.** Write the part of speech for each word. Then complete the sentences with the words. Use the dictionary to help you.

a. architect _____

b. architecture _____

c. lecturer _____

d. lecture _____

e. recent _____

f. recently _____

g. variety _____

h. various _____

Matt designs buildings.

The restaurants in China were all great.

1. Matt designs buildings. He is a(n) _____.

2. I tried _____ restaurants in China, and they were all great.

3. In Cairo, we visited a(n) _____ of monuments.

4. Toshi _____ returned from Tokyo.

5. The _____ from the college gave a very interesting talk on the history of Saudi Arabia.

6. I want to study the _____ in Istanbul. The buildings there are beautiful.

7. Mary is a wonderful public speaker. She wants to _____ at universities.

8. I met Carlos on my _____ trip to Rio.

 **C.** Go online for more practice with using a dictionary.

# SPEAKING

**At the end of this unit, you are going to give a presentation about a special city.**

| Grammar | Past of *be*; Simple past affirmative statements |
| --- | --- |

**Past of *be***

Use the past of *be* to identify and describe people and things in the past.

| Affirmative and negative statements | | | |
| --- | --- | --- | --- |
| subject | *be* | *(not)* | |
| I | **was** | | very happy. |
| You<br>We<br>They | **were** | **(not)** | busy yesterday. |
| He<br>She<br>It | **was** | | in Ubud last week. |

- You can contract negative statements:

  was not = wasn't      were not = weren't

- Past time expressions answer the question, *When?*

  **last** + time:      last week, last month
  time + **ago**:      three days **ago**, one year **ago**

| Yes / No questions | | | Short answers | |
| --- | --- | --- | --- | --- |
| *be* | subject | | *yes* | *no* |
| **Was** | he | in China? | Yes, he **was**. | No, he **wasn't**. |
| **Were** | they | excited? | Yes, they **were**. | No, they **weren't**. |

| Information questions | | | Answers |
| --- | --- | --- | --- |
| *wh-* word | *be* | subject | |
| **How** | were | Paris and Rome? | They **were** great! |
| **What** | was | your favorite city? | Istanbul **was** my favorite city. |
| **When** | was | the lecture? | The lecture **was** last week. |

## Simple past affirmative statements

The simple past describes completed actions in the past.

Regular past verbs end in -ed. The simple past form is the same for all subjects.

> I **visited** Brazil last year.
> They **liked** their trip to Tokyo.
> He **shopped** downtown yesterday.
> We **stayed** at a nice hotel.

| Spelling simple past verbs | | |
|---|---|---|
| like–lik**ed** | stay–stay**ed** | try–tr**ied** |
| shop–shop**ped** | travel–travel**ed** | visit–visit**ed** |

**A.** Put the words in the correct order. Use the correct simple past form of *be* in each question. Then ask and answer the questions with a partner.

1. you / where / yesterday / be ?

   _____

2. last week / be / you / on vacation ?

   _____

3. be / last trip / how / your ?

   _____

4. last vacation / it / be / on / your / cold ?

   _____

5. be / when you were young / what / your favorite city ?

   _____

6. in this city / you / be / last year ?

   _____

**B.** Complete Sarah's email about her trip to Istanbul. Use the past form of the words in the box.

| shop | stay | travel | try | visit | walk |

To: annatwo@email.org
From: sarahfive@email.org
Subject: My trip to Istanbul

Dear Anna,

    I'm back from my vacation! I _____ to Istanbul last month. My trip
                      1
was so much fun! I _____ in a really nice hotel. There was a view of
                 2
a beautiful park outside my window. I _____ a lot of great museums.
                        3
I also _____ around the city every day. The food was delicious. I
            4
_____ baklava for the first time. It's a dessert made with nuts and
        5
syrup. On my last day, I _____ at a big market. There were so many
                   6
pretty scarves, shoes, and bags. Let's get together soon. I have a gift for you!

See you soon!

Sarah

the Grand Bazaar in Istanbul

**C.** Write about a city you visited. Complete the sentences. Then read your sentences to a partner.

1. I traveled to _____.

2. I visited _____.

3. I tried _____.

4. I loved _____.

5. I stayed _____.

6. There was / were _____.

**D.** Go online for more practice with the past of *be* and simple past affirmative statements.

**E.** Go online for the grammar expansion.

There are three ways to pronounce the *-ed* ending of a simple past verb.

| /t/ | | /d/ | | /ɪd/ | |
|---|---|---|---|---|---|
| walk**ed** | lik**ed** | travel**ed** | lov**ed** | visit**ed** | want**ed** |

**A.** Listen to the sentences. Circle the sound that you hear at the end of the verb. Then practice the sentences with a partner.

**They collected shells.**

1. They collected shells on the beach in Oman.          /t/     /d/     /ɪd/
2. We tried to go to the Natural History Museum.      /t/     /d/     /ɪd/
3. He shopped all afternoon.                          /t/     /d/     /ɪd/
4. We started our tour at noon.                       /t/     /d/     /ɪd/
5. I worked in Dubai last year.                       /t/     /d/     /ɪd/
6. Heavy traffic caused problems in Los Angeles.      /t/     /d/     /ɪd/

**B.** Write four sentences about a special city. Use verbs from the box.

| enjoyed | needed | shopped | stayed | visited |
|---|---|---|---|---|
| liked | relaxed | started | tried | wanted |

1. _____
2. _____
3. _____
4. _____

**C.** Read your sentences from Activity B to a partner. Circle the sounds you hear in your partner's sentences.

| **1.** /t/     /d/     /ɪd/ | **3.** /t/     /d/     /ɪd/ |
|---|---|
| **2.** /t/     /d/     /ɪd/ | **4.** /t/     /d/     /ɪd/ |

   **D.** Go online for more practice with *-ed* endings.

Look at the two conversations below. In Conversation 1, Isabel asks a **closed question** (a *yes / no* question), and Sun-Hee answers "Yes." In Conversation 2, Isabel asks an **open question** (a *wh-* question). Sun-Hee gives her more information. Open questions make a conversation more interesting.

| Conversation 1: Closed question | Conversation 2: Open question |
|---|---|
| **A:** I visited Hong Kong last week. | **A:** I visited Hong Kong last week. |
| **B: Was it fun?** | **B: How was it?** |
| **A:** Yes. | **A:** It was great. I visited a lot of interesting sights, and I tried new food. |

**A.** **Listen to the conversation. Complete the questions. Then practice with a partner.**

the Acropolis in Athens

**Emma:** John, _____ Greece?
<sub>1</sub>

**John:** Fantastic! I liked Athens a lot. The museums and architecture were great. And the view from the top of the Acropolis was amazing!

**Emma:** _____?
<sub>2</sub>

**John:** Well, Greeks eat a lot of bread, cheese, olives, and vegetables. For meat, they eat a lot of lamb. I love all of those foods, so I was very happy!

**Emma:** That sounds great, John.

**John:** _____ your trip to Mexico City?
<sub>3</sub>

**Emma:** It was good, but I was really busy.

traffic in Mexico City

**John:** That's too bad. _____ Mexico City _____?
<sub>4</sub>                <sub>5</sub>

**Emma:** Well, it's huge! It's very busy, and the traffic is sometimes awful.

**John:** Uh-huh. _____ the food?
<sub>6</sub>

**Emma:** It was delicious. We had fresh vegetables and fruit every day.

**John:** That's great!

**B.** Look at the sentences you wrote in Grammar Activity C on page 130. Discuss your trip with a partner. Use open questions to find out more information.

A: *I traveled to Seoul last year.*

B: *What was it like?*

A: *It was fantastic. Seoul is a beautiful city. I visited…*

 **C.** Go online for more practice with using open questions.

---

**Unit Assignment** **Give a presentation about a special city**

 In this assignment, you are going to choose a special city and give a presentation about it. Think about the Unit Question, "What makes a city special?" Use Listening 1, Listening 2, the unit video, and your work in this unit. Look at the Self-Assessment checklist on page 134.

## CONSIDER THE IDEAS

What does this advertisement show about London? Check (✓) the things on page 134. Then share with a partner.

| | |
|---|---|
| ☐ 1. interesting sights | ☐ 8. job opportunities |
| ☐ 2. good shopping | ☐ 9. friendly residents |
| ☐ 3. natural beauty | ☐ 10. culture |
| ☐ 4. great museums | ☐ 11. a variety of restaurants |
| ☐ 5. beautiful architecture | ☐ 12. beautiful views |
| ☐ 6. historic buildings | ☐ 13. clean and safe parks |
| ☐ 7. important monuments | ☐ 14. good public transportation |

## PREPARE AND SPEAK

**A. FIND IDEAS** Work with a group of four. Think of a list of special cities. Why is each city special? Take notes.

**B. ORGANIZE IDEAS** With your group, look at your notes from Activity A.

- Choose only one city to present to the class. Why is this city special? Write three or four reasons.
- Describe an experience you had there. What did you do? Where did you go?
- If you want, cut out or print photos of your city. Make an advertisement like the one on page 133.
- Each person chooses a reason to describe and gives information about an experience there.
- Practice your presentation.

**C. SPEAK** Take turns presenting information about your city. Look at the Self-Assessment checklist below before you begin.

 Go online for your alternate Unit Assignment.

 **Tip for Success**

Remember: Give extra information to make your presentation more interesting.

## CHECK AND REFLECT

**A. CHECK** Think about the Unit Assignment as you complete the Self-Assessment checklist.

| SELF-ASSESSMENT | | |
|---|---|---|
| Yes | No | |
| ☐ | ☐ | My information was clear. |
| ☐ | ☐ | I used vocabulary from this unit. |
| ☐ | ☐ | I used the past tense correctly. |
| ☐ | ☐ | I pronounced past tense verbs with -ed correctly. |
| ☐ | ☐ | I asked open questions during our discussions. |

**B.** **REFLECT** Go to the Online Discussion Board to discuss these questions.

1. What is something new you learned in this unit?

2. Think about the Unit Question—What makes a city special? Do you have a different opinion now? If yes, how is your opinion different? Why?

# TRACK YOUR SUCCESS

**Circle the words you have learned in this unit.**

**Nouns**
architect
climate 🔑
correction
culture 🔑 AWL
lecture AWL
lecturer AWL
location AWL
monument
opportunity 🔑
resident AWL
sight 🔑

skyscraper
variety 🔑
view 🔑

**Adjectives**
average 🔑
correct 🔑
historic
located AWL
recent 🔑
special 🔑
various 🔑

**Verbs**
correct 🔑
create 🔑 AWL
improve 🔑
locate AWL
specialize

**Adverbs**
correctly 🔑
recently 🔑
specially

🔑 Oxford 2000 keywords
AWL Academic Word List

**Check (✓) the skills you learned. If you need more work on a skill, refer to the page(s) in parentheses.**

| | |
|---|---|
| **NOTE TAKING** ☐ | I can take notes in an informal outline. (p. 116) |
| **LISTENING** ☐ | I can identify frequency words and expressions. (p. 120) |
| **VOCABULARY** ☐ | I can use the dictionary to identify word families. (p. 126) |
| **GRAMMAR** ☐ | I can use the past of *be* and simple past affirmative statements. (p. 128) |
| **PRONUNCIATION** ☐ | I can pronounce *-ed* endings. (p. 131) |
| **SPEAKING** ☐ | I can use open questions. (p. 132) |
| **UNIT OBJECTIVE** ▶▶▶▶ ☐ | I can use information and ideas to give a presentation about a special city. |

UNIT **8**

Developmental Psychology

| NOTE TAKING | ▶ | taking notes in a timeline |
| LISTENING | ▶ | listening for sequence |
| VOCABULARY | ▶ | phrases with *get* |
| GRAMMAR | ▶ | simple past with regular and irregular verbs |
| PRONUNCIATION | ▶ | numbers with *-teen* and *-ty* |
| SPEAKING | ▶ | review: using open questions |

**UNIT QUESTION**

# What are the most important events in someone's life?

**A** Discuss these questions with your classmates.

1. Look at the photos. What important events do you see?

2. What events are important to you? Complete the statements. Add one more event.

   a. I was born in _____ (year) in _____ (place).

   b. I started studying English when I was _____ years old.

   c. I traveled to _____ when I was _____ years old.

   d. _____

Listen to a radio program and a class presentation.
Use information and ideas to interview a classmate
about important life events. Then present him or her
to the class.

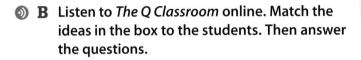

**B** Listen to *The Q Classroom* online. Match the
ideas in the box to the students. Then answer
the questions.

a. getting your first job
b. getting my first soccer ball
c. starting college
d. getting my driver's license

| Important events | |
|---|---|
| Yuna | |
| Marcus | |
| Sophy | a. getting your first job |
| Felix | |

1. Did the students have different answers from yours?

2. How old do you think the students are? Why do you think so?

**C** Go to the Online Discussion Board to discuss the Unit Question
with your classmates.

A **timeline** is a list of important events and the times that they happened. You can take notes in a timeline to list the order of events. Look at the sample timeline of Lina's life.

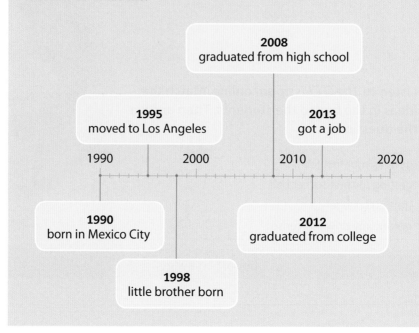

**2008**
graduated from high school

**1995**
moved to Los Angeles

**2013**
got a job

1990          2000          2010          2020

**1990**
born in Mexico City

**2012**
graduated from college

**1998**
little brother born

**A.** Listen to two people talk about the life of Nelson Mandela. Then complete the timeline.

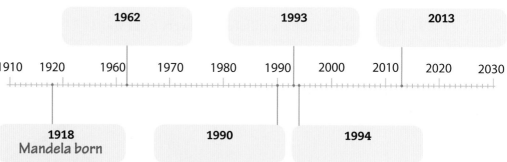

**1962**          **1993**          **2013**

1910    1920      1960    1970    1980    1990    2000    2010    2020    2030

**1918**
Mandela born

**1990**          **1994**

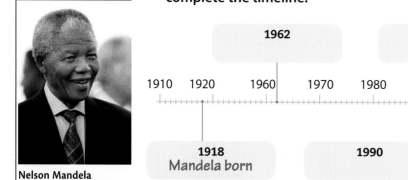

Nelson Mandela

**B.** Go online for more practice taking notes in a timeline.

# LISTENING

## LISTENING 1 | Henrietta Leavitt: Understanding the Stars

**UNIT OBJECTIVE** ▶▶▶▶ You are going to listen to a radio program about a scientist who made an important discovery. Think about the most important events in someone's life.

## PREVIEW THE LISTENING

genius

**A. VOCABULARY** Here are some words from Listening 1. Read the sentences. Which explanation is correct? Circle *a* or *b*.

1. Jena is a mathematical <u>genius</u>. She's very young, but she can do difficult math problems.
   a. Jena has difficulty in school.
   b. Jena is extremely intelligent.

2. Mary is an <u>astronomer</u>. She spends many nights looking at the sky.
   a. Mary is a kind of scientist.
   b. Mary is a kind of writer.

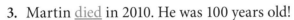
astronomer

3. Martin <u>died</u> in 2010. He was 100 years old!
   a. Martin stopped living in 2010.
   b. Martin began living in 2010.

4. There are millions of <u>stars</u> in the sky at night! The sun is the closest star to Earth.
   a. A star is the same thing as a planet.
   b. A star is a large ball of burning gas a long way from us.

5. <u>Brightness</u> changes for different stars. Some give off a lot of light, but others are difficult to see from Earth.
   a. Brightness is how much light something gives off.
   b. Brightness is how big something is.

6. The <u>distance</u> between the cities of Dallas and Fort Worth is very small. You can drive from downtown Dallas to downtown Fort Worth in about 30 minutes.
   a. Dallas is far from Fort Worth.
   b. Dallas is near Fort Worth.

7. Benjamin Franklin <u>discovered</u> important facts about electricity. He showed that lightning is electricity.
   a. He read about electricity and understood the facts.
   b. He found new information about electricity.

8. The <u>universe</u> is really big! It contains planets, stars, and moons.
   a. The universe is Earth, our moon, and the sun.
   b. The universe is everything that exists.

**B.** Go online for more practice with the vocabulary.

**Tip for Success**

A *milestone* is an important event in someone's life.

**C.** **PREVIEW** You are going to listen to a radio program about Henrietta Leavitt, a scientist. You will hear many milestones from her life.

Henrietta Leavitt

1. Who do you think is a genius? What makes him or her a genius?

2. What famous scientists do you know of? Write down at least four names.

## WORK WITH THE LISTENING

**A.** Listen to the radio program. Answer the questions.

1. What kind of scientist was Henrietta Leavitt?
   a. biologist
   b. chemist
   c. astronomer

2. What was her big discovery?
   a. the size of stars
   b. the brightness of stars
   c. the number of stars

3. How does Dr. Watkins describe Leavitt?
   a. hard working and smart
   b. sad and intelligent
   c. famous and hard working

4. What do we know now because of Leavitt's work?
   a. All stars are really bright.
   b. The universe is really big.
   c. There are millions of stars.

**B. Listen again. Write the milestone for each year.**

1868 _____

1892 _____

1893 _____

1912 _____

1921 _____

**C. Complete the timeline with information from Activity B.**

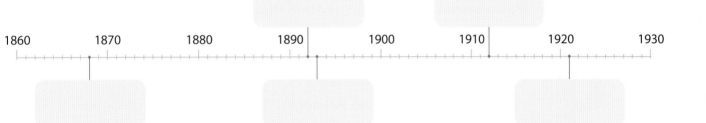

**D. Listen again. Circle the best answer to complete each sentence.**

1. Leavitt was born in ____.
   a. New Hampshire
   b. New York
   c. Massachusetts
   d. Maine

2. Leavitt went to school at ____.
   a. Radcliffe College
   b. the University of Massachusetts
   c. the University of California
   d. Harvard University

3. Leavitt got a job at ___.
   a. Yale University
   b. the University of Massachusetts
   c. the University of California
   d. Harvard University

4. Leavitt studied ___ of stars.
   a. the distance
   b. the brightness
   c. the size
   d. the length

5. Other scientists discovered the ___ because of Leavitt's work.
   a. distance of stars from the Earth
   b. number of stars in the universe
   c. size of stars in the universe
   d. brightness of stars in the sky

**E.** Go online to listen to *Author Mario Vargas Llosa* and check your comprehension.

## SAY WHAT YOU THINK

**A.** Do you agree with these statements? Write *A* (agree) or *D* (disagree).

___ 1. Harvard University treated Henrietta Leavitt fairly.

___ 2. Geniuses are different from other people.

___ 3. Everyone should study astronomy.

___ 4. Everyone is born with special talents.

___ 5. Schools should help all students find their talents.

___ 6. Parents should help their children find their talents.

**B.** Discuss your answers with a partner. Give reasons for your opinions.

Two or more events happen in a **sequence**. First one thing happens. Then another thing happens. These words and expressions can help you listen for sequence.

Sam was born **in 1992**. His family lived in Egypt, but they moved a lot.
**First**, they moved to Chile.
**Then** they lived in Singapore.
**When Sam was 12**, his family went to Shanghai.
**Finally**, they moved to Seoul. They live there now.

**A. Listen to the conversation. Number the events in the correct order (1–6).**

___ a.   Her family moved to Boston, Massachusetts.

___ b.   She got a job in a store in San Francisco, California.

_1_ c.   John's grandmother was born in Jamestown, New York.

___ d.   Her family lived in Philadelphia, Pennsylvania.

___ e.   Her family moved to Miami, Florida.

___ f.   She moved to Los Angeles, California.

John and his grandmother

**B. Listen to parts of the conversation again. Circle the expressions you hear.**

| | | |
|---|---|---|
| **1.** first | in 1950 | then |
| **2.** in 1955 | first | when I was a teenager |
| **3.** when I was ten | in 1960 | then |
| **4.** when I was 18 | then | in 1968 |
| **5.** in 1972 | finally | when I was 22 |
| **6.** finally | then | in 1980 |

 **C.** Go online for more practice listening for sequence.

**UNIT OBJECTIVE** ▶▶ ▶▶

You are going to listen to a presentation about a writer. Think about the most important events in someone's life.

## PREVIEW THE LISTENING

**A.** **VOCABULARY** Here are some words from Listening 2. Read the definitions. Then complete each sentence.

---

**attend** (*verb*) to go to a place, especially a school

**government** (*noun*) 🔑 the group of people who rule a country

**graduate** (*verb*) to finish your studies at school (usually high school or college)

**literature** (*noun*) 🔑 books, plays, and poetry

**novel** (*noun*) 🔑 a book about people and things that are not real

**politics** (*noun*) 🔑 work and ideas connected with government

**retire** (*verb*) to stop working because you are a certain age

---

🔑 Oxford 2000 keywords

Jose's students read a lot of books.

1. Jose teaches _____. His students read a lot of books.

2. Sam works for the Canadian _____. He meets a lot of world leaders.

3. Adel wants to _____ from his company next March when he turns 65 years old.

4. Sarah _____ Boston University. She takes classes there.

5. My favorite _____ is *A Tale of Two Cities* by Charles Dickens. I read it every year.

6. There are always a lot of stories about _____ in the news. Today there was a story about the new president of Mexico.

7. Rasha plans to _____ from college this year. She should start looking for a job.

**B. Answer these questions. Then ask and answer the questions with a partner.**

1. What high school did (or do) you attend? _____

2. When did you (or will you) graduate from high school? _____

3. Do you enjoy reading literature? _____

4. What is your favorite novel? _____

**C.** Go online for more practice with the vocabulary.

**D.** **PREVIEW** You are going to listen to a presentation about Naguib Mahfouz (pronounced *na-HEEB ma-FOOS*), a famous writer. Before listening, discuss these questions with a partner.

1. Who is your favorite writer? Why is this writer your favorite?

2. What are the Nobel Prizes?

**Naguib Mahfouz**

# WORK WITH THE LISTENING

**A.** Read the questions. Listen to the people. Then circle the correct answers.

1. Where are the people?
   a. in an office
   b. in a store
   c. in a classroom
   d. in a house

2. What are the people doing?
   a. listening to a student presentation
   b. reading reports on famous people
   c. discussing political topics
   d. listening to their professor

3. What does Hassan talk about?
   a. the history of Egypt
   b. the Nobel Prize
   c. the novel *Palace Walk*
   d. the writer Naguib Mahfouz

**B.** Read the sentences. Then listen again. Write *T* (true) or *F* (false) for each sentence. Then correct each false statement to make it true.

_____ 1. Naguib Mahfouz grew up in Cairo.

_____ 2. He came from a large family.

_____ 3. His mother took him to parks.

_____ 4. His father was a government employee.

_____ 5. He worked for the Egyptian government.

_____ 6. He had three children.

_____ 7. He wrote only a few novels.

_____ 8. He wrote for 70 years.

**C.** Read the questions. Circle the correct answers.

1. What novel by Naguib Mahfouz does Hassan mention?
   a. *Parting Talk*      c. *Parents' Park*
   b. *Palace Walk*      d. *Plant Talk*

2. What two subjects was Naguib Mahfouz interested in as a child?
   a. history and literature      c. history and politics
   b. literature and politics      d. mathematics and history

3. In what year did he graduate from college?
   a. 1904      c. 1923
   b. 1913      d. 1934

4. How old was he when he got married?
   a. 23      c. 34
   b. 32      d. 43

5. How many novels did he write?
   a. 23      c. 34
   b. 32      d. 43

6. Which Nobel Prize did he win?
   a. History      c. Literature
   b. Peace      d. Politics

7. How old was he when he died?
   a. 64      c. 84
   b. 74      d. 94

**D.** Listen to the conversation again. Number the events in the correct order (1–7).

____ His mother took him to museums.

____ He got married.

____ He retired from the Ministry of Culture.

____ He graduated from Cairo University.

____ He died at the age of 94.

_1_ Naguib Mahfouz was born in Cairo, Egypt.

____ He won the Nobel Prize for Literature.

**SAY WHAT YOU THINK**

**A.** What were some milestones in your life? Check (✓) them below. Add one more idea. Then discuss with a partner.

**Critical Thinking** (Tip)

In Activity A, you **choose** your important milestones. *Choosing* means you have to make decisions. You use your own experiences and knowledge to make choices.

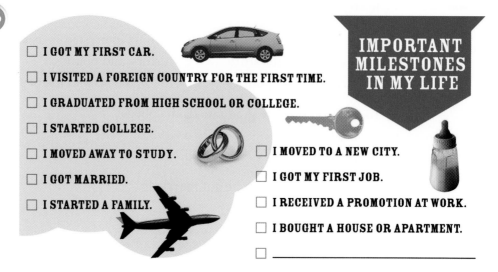

**IMPORTANT MILESTONES IN MY LIFE**

- ☐ I GOT MY FIRST CAR.
- ☐ I VISITED A FOREIGN COUNTRY FOR THE FIRST TIME.
- ☐ I GRADUATED FROM HIGH SCHOOL OR COLLEGE.
- ☐ I STARTED COLLEGE.
- ☐ I MOVED AWAY TO STUDY.
- ☐ I GOT MARRIED.
- ☐ I STARTED A FAMILY.
- ☐ I MOVED TO A NEW CITY.
- ☐ I GOT MY FIRST JOB.
- ☐ I RECEIVED A PROMOTION AT WORK.
- ☐ I BOUGHT A HOUSE OR APARTMENT.
- ☐ _____

**B.** Before you watch the video, answer these questions in a group.

1. Should very young geniuses study with children their age?

2. How old should someone be to go to college?

**iQ** ONLINE

**C.** Go online to watch a video about a genius. Then check your comprehension.

> **cancer** *(n.)* a very dangerous disease that makes very small parts in the body (cells) grow too fast
>
> **exam** *(n.)* a test
>
> **grade** *(n.)* a class level, for example, 4th grade

VIDEO VOCABULARY

**D.** Think about the video, Listening 1, and Listening 2. Then discuss these questions in a group.

1. What are the biggest milestones in people's lives?

2. What was your first important milestone?

3. What was your most recent milestone?

4. What were the two most important milestones in your life? Why were they important?

There are many phrases with the word *get*. In these phrases, *get* often means *receive* or *become*. The past tense form of *get* is *got*.

> John **got married** in 2009.
> Anna **got a job** at a big company.

| More phrases with *get* | | |
|---|---|---|
| get along | get hurt/injured | get lost |
| get better/worse | get in touch | get sick |
| get engaged | get in trouble | |
| get hired | get laid off (lose a job) | |

**Ahmed and Feride**

**A. Complete the sentences. Use a phrase with *get* in the simple past.**

1. Ahmed and Feride _____ in 2001. Now they have two children.

2. Miteb _____ last week. He has a terrible cold.

3. Sun-Hee _____ at work because she was late yesterday. Her boss said, "Don't be late again!"

4. Sam and Anna _____ last night. Their wedding will be in June.

5. James _____ because his company had a lot of problems. He is now looking for a new job.

6. Kayo _____ with an old friend yesterday. She bumped into her in the park.

7. Emma _____ at work. She broke her leg.

8. Rob and Sam _____ well when they were young. But they aren't friends now.

9. We _____ on our way to the museum. We

don't know this city very well.

10. James _____. Now he is a manager at

a restaurant.

James is a manager now.

**B.** Complete the sentences about yourself, a friend, or a family member. Then discuss with a partner.

1. _____ got engaged _____.

2. _____ got married _____.

3. _____ got laid off _____.

4. _____ got hired _____.

5. _____ got a job _____.

6. _____ got injured _____.

 **C.** Go online for more practice using phrases with *get*.

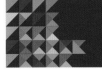

# SPEAKING

 **UNIT OBJECTIVE** At the end of this unit, you are going to give a presentation about important milestones in a classmate's life.

| Grammar | Simple past with regular and irregular verbs |
|---|---|

The simple past describes completed actions in the past.

> I **graduated** from college two years ago.
> I **started** playing tennis when I was ten years old.

Many verbs have irregular past forms. They don't end in -ed.

### Irregular past forms

| begin | **began** | eat | **ate** | have | **had** | read | **read** |
|---|---|---|---|---|---|---|---|
| buy | **bought** | get | **got** | make | **made** | see | **saw** |
| come | **came** | go | **went** | meet | **met** | take | **took** |
| do | **did** | grow | **grew** | put | **put** | think | **thought** |

### Affirmative statements

| subject | verb | |
|---|---|---|
| I / You / We / They | **moved** | to Chile last year. |
| He / She / It | **came** | at noon yesterday. |

- For affirmative statements, use the same past form for all subjects.

### Negative statements

| subject | did + not | verb | |
|---|---|---|---|
| I / You / We / They | **did not** | **move** | to Chile. |
| He / She / It | **didn't** | **come** | yesterday. |

- For negative statements, use *did not* + the base verb for both regular and irregular verbs.

| Yes / No questions | | | | Short answers | |
|---|---|---|---|---|---|
| *did* | subject | verb | | *yes* | *no* |
| **Did** | you | **get** | a new job? | Yes, I **did.** | No, I **didn't.** |
| | he | **like** | the novel? | Yes, he **did.** | No, he **didn't.** |

| Information questions | | | | | Answers |
|---|---|---|---|---|---|
| *wh-* word | *did* | subject | verb | | past verb |
| **Where** | | you | **go** | to school? | I **went** to school in Tokyo. |
| **When** | **did** | he | **start** | his new job? | He **started** last Saturday. |
| **What** | | they | **buy?** | | They **bought** a new car. |

**A.** Complete each sentence. Use the correct simple past form. Some sentences are negative.

Ian has a new car.

1. James _____ (not / go) to Beijing last year.

2. Emma _____ (eat) a delicious meal at the new restaurant.

3. Kate and Matt _____ (have) a baby in November.

4. Ian _____ (buy) a new car yesterday.

5. Carlos _____ (not / get) laid off from his job.

6. Turki _____ (not / graduate) from college in June.

7. May _____ (take) a cooking class.

8. Amal _____ (retire) from teaching two years ago.

9. Sun-Hee _____ (not / give) Anna a book yesterday.

10. Lisa _____ (become) a doctor three years ago.

**B.** Look at the underlined information in the answers below. What question does the information answer—*when, what, where,* or *why*? Write a question for each answer.

Anita called me yesterday.

1. Question:_____

   Answer: Anita called me <u>yesterday.</u>

2. Question:_____

   Answer: He got lost <u>because he didn't have a map</u>.

**3.** Question:_____

Answer: He went <u>to Shanghai</u> for vacation.

**4.** Question:_____

Answer: He bought his son <u>a bicycle</u> as a present.

**C.** **What did you do yesterday? What <u>didn't</u> you do? Write sentences. Use the verbs in the box. Then read your sentences to a partner.**

| buy | do | give | have | read | study |
|-----|-----|------|------|------|-------|
| come | eat | go | play | see | watch |

**Things I did**

**1.** _____

**2.** _____

**Things I didn't do**

**3.** _____

**4.** _____

**D.** Go online for more practice with the simple past.

**E.** Go online for the grammar expansion.

**Pronunciation** Numbers with *-teen* and *-ty*

Numbers ending in *-teen* (*13* and *14*) and numbers ending in *-ty* (*30* and *40*) can be difficult to pronounce. These numbers sound similar, but you pronounce the second syllable differently.

| Numbers with *-teen* | Numbers with *-ty* |
|---|---|
| The second syllable starts with a hard "t" sound and ends with "n." | The second syllable uses a soft "d" sound, like "dee." |
| 13 "thir-teen" | 30 "thir-dee" |
| 14 "four-teen" | 40 "four-dee" |
| 15 "fif-teen" | 50 "fif-dee" |

**A.** Listen to the sentences. Circle the number that you hear. Then practice the sentences with a partner.

1. My cousin is ( 13 / 30 ) years old.

2. She was born in ( 1916 / 1960 ).

3. The shirt cost ( 15 / 50 ) dollars.

4. She graduated at the age of ( 18 / 80 ).

5. The president died in ( 1913 / 1930 ).

6. The plane ticket was ( 414 / 440 ) dollars.

7. His great-grandfather was born in ( 1914 / 1940 ).

8. The train left at ( 4:15 / 4:50 ).

The train left at...

**B.** For each item, write a sentence with one of the numbers. Then read your sentences to a partner. Listen to your partner's sentences. What number do you hear?

**Tip for Success**

If you don't understand a number, you can ask a question like, "Did you say *thirteen—one-three?"*

1. ( 13 / 30 ) _____

2. ( 14 / 40 ) _____

3. ( 15 / 50 ) _____

4. ( 16 / 60 ) _____

5. ( 17 / 70 ) _____

**C.** Go online for more practice with numbers with *-teen* and *-ty.*

In this assignment, you are going to interview a classmate and give a presentation. Think about the Unit Question, "What are the most important events in someone's life?" Use Listening 1, Listening 2, the unit video, and your work in this unit. Look at the Self-Assessment checklist on page 156.

## CONSIDER THE IDEAS

Read the sentences about the milestones in Toshi's life. Match each milestone with the correct detail.

| Milestones | Details |
|---|---|
| 1. Toshi's family moved to Tokyo. ___ | a. He got stronger and faster, and he made a lot of friends on his soccer team. |
| 2. He joined a soccer team in middle school. ___ | b. He studied computer engineering, and he learned a lot from his professors. |
| 3. His grandfather died. ___ | c. He was Toshi's best friend. He always had time to talk to Toshi. |
| 4. He started taking tennis lessons. ___ | d. Tokyo had good middle schools. His old city didn't have good schools. |
| 5. He started college in Osaka. ___ | e. He made new friends from different countries, and his English improved a lot. |
| 6. He came to London to study English. ___ | f. He really enjoyed learning something new. He still plays tennis a lot. |

Toshi

---

**Skill Review** | Using open questions

Remember: Ask open questions to get answers with more information. Review the Speaking Skill box in Unit 7 on page 132.

A: In 2006, I went to India.
B: What was it like?

A: I came to this school last year.
B: Why did you choose this school?

# PREPARE AND SPEAK

**A.** `FIND IDEAS` Interview your partner. Follow these steps.

1. Start with a general question like, "What were the important events in your life?"

2. Ask follow-up questions for details and reasons, for example, "When did that happen?" and "Why was that important?"

3. Get information about at least six milestones. Draw a timeline and record your partner's milestones and details.

**B.** `ORGANIZE IDEAS` Choose four of your partner's milestones to present to your class.

- Make an outline for your presentation.
- Include at least two details about each milestone.

**C.** `SPEAK` Tell your class about your partner's milestones. Look at the Self-Assessment checklist below before you begin.

 Go online for your alternate Unit Assignment.

# CHECK AND REFLECT

**A.** `CHECK` Think about the Unit Assignment as you complete the Self-Assessment checklist.

| SELF-ASSESSMENT | | |
|:---:|:---:|:---|
| Yes | No | |
| ☐ | ☐ | My information was clear. |
| ☐ | ☐ | I drew a clear timeline. |
| ☐ | ☐ | I used vocabulary from this unit. |
| ☐ | ☐ | I used the past tense correctly. |
| ☐ | ☐ | I used expressions with *get* correctly. |
| ☐ | ☐ | I pronounced numbers correctly. |

 **B.** `REFLECT` Go to the Online Discussion Board to discuss these questions.

1. What is something new you learned in this unit?

2. Think about the Unit Question—What are the most important events in someone's life? Is your answer different now than when you started this unit? If yes, how is it different? Why?

# TRACK YOUR SUCCESS

Circle the words and phrases you have learned in this unit.

| Nouns | Verb | Phrases |
|---|---|---|
| astronomer | attend | get along |
| brightness | die 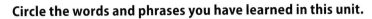 | get better/worse |
| distance | discover | get engaged |
| genius | graduate | get hired |
| government | retire | get hurt/injured |
| literature | | get in touch |
| novel | | get in trouble |
| politics | | get a job |
| star | | get laid off |
| universe | | get lost |
| | | get married |
| | | get sick |

Oxford 2000 keywords

AWL  Academic Word List

Check (✓) the skills you learned. If you need more work on a skill, refer to the page(s) in parentheses.

| | |
|---|---|
| **NOTE TAKING** | ☐ I can take notes using a timeline. (p. 138) |
| **LISTENING** | ☐ I can identify a sequence. (p. 143) |
| **VOCABULARY** | ☐ I can understand many phrases with *get*. (p. 149) |
| **GRAMMAR** | ☐ I can use the simple past with regular and irregular verbs. (p. 151) |
| **PRONUNCIATION** | ☐ I can pronounce numbers with *-teen* and *-ty*. (p. 153) |
| **SPEAKING** | ☐ I can use open questions. (p. 155) |
| **UNIT OBJECTIVE** ▶▶▶▶ | ☐ I can use information and ideas to interview a classmate and give a presentation. |

Audio can be found in the *iQ Online* Media Center. Go to iQOnlinePractice.com. Click on the Media Center Choose to stream or download ⬇ the audio file you select. Not all audio files are available for download.

| Page | Track Name: Q2e_00_LS_ | Page | Track Name: Q2e_00_LS_ |
|---|---|---|---|
| 2 | U01_Q_Classroom.mp3 | 71 | U05_Q_Classroom.mp3 |
| 6 | U01_Listening_ActivityA.mp3 | 73 | U05_Listening1_ActivityA.mp3 |
| 6 | U01_Listening_ActivityB.mp3 | 74 | U05_Listening1_ActivityC.mp3 |
| 7 | U01_Listening_ActivityD.mp3 | 76 | U05_ListeningSkill_Examples.mp3 |
| 8 | U01_BuildingVocabulary_ActivityA.mp3 | 77 | U05_ListeningSkill_ActivityA.mp3 |
| 8 | U01_BuildingVocabulary_ActivityB.mp3 | 78 | U05_NoteTakingSkill_ActivityA.mp3 |
| 13 | U01_Pronunciation_Examples.mp3 | 80 | U05_Listening2_ActivityA.mp3 |
| 13 | U01_Pronunciation_ActivityA.mp3 | 82 | U05_Listening2_ActivityC.mp3 |
| 14 | U01_SpeakingSkill_Example1.mp3 | 84 | U05_Pronunciation_Examples.mp3 |
| 15 | U01_SpeakingSkill_Example2.mp3 | 84 | U05_Pronunciation_ActivityA.mp3 |
| 15 | U01_SpeakingSkill_ActivityB.mp3 | 89 | U05_UnitAssignment.mp3 |
| 17 | U01_UnitAssignment.mp3 | | |
| | | 92 | U06_Q_Classroom.mp3 |
| 21 | U02_Q_Classroom.mp3 | 95 | U06_Listening1_ActivityA.mp3 |
| 24 | U02_Listening_ActivityA.mp3 | 96 | U06_Listening1_ActivityB.mp3 |
| 25 | U02_ListeningSkill_Examples.mp3 | 96 | U06_Listening1_ActivityC.mp3 |
| 25 | U02_ListeningSkill_ActivityC.mp3 | 98 | U06_ListeningSkill_Examples.mp3 |
| 26 | U02_NoteTakingSkill_Examples.mp3 | 98 | U06_ListeningSkill_ActivityA.mp3 |
| 26 | U02_NoteTakingSkill_ActivityA.mp3 | 99 | U06_ListeningSkill_ActivityB.mp3 |
| 31 | U02_Pronunciation_Examples.mp3 | 100 | U06_NoteTakingSkill_ActivityA.mp3 |
| 31 | U02_Pronunciation_ActivityA.mp3 | 102 | U06_Listening2_ActivityA.mp3 |
| 32 | U02_SpeakingSkill_Examples.mp3 | 102 | U06_Listening2_ActivityB.mp3 |
| 32 | U02_SpeakingSkill_ActivityA.mp3 | 108 | U06_Pronunciation_Examples.mp3 |
| 33 | U02_UnitAssignment.mp3 | 109 | U06_Pronunciation_ActivityA.mp3 |
| | | 110 | U06_SpeakingSkill_ActivityA.mp3 |
| 37 | U03_Q_Classroom.mp3 | 111 | U06_UnitAssignment.mp3 |
| 40 | U03_Listening_ActivityA.mp3 | | |
| 40 | U03_Listening_ActivityB.mp3 | 114 | U07_Q_Classroom.mp3 |
| 43 | U03_Pronunciation_Examples.mp3 | 118 | U07_Listening1_ActivityA.mp3 |
| 43 | U03_Pronunciation_ActivityA.mp3 | 119 | U07_Listening1_ActivityB.mp3 |
| 44 | U03_Pronunciation_ActivityB.mp3 | 121 | U07_SkillReview_ActivityF.mp3 |
| 44 | U03_Pronunciation_ActivityC.mp3 | 123 | U07_Listening2_ActivityA.mp3 |
| 44 | U03_ListeningSkill_Examples.mp3 | 124 | U07_Listening2_ActivityB.mp3 |
| 44 | U03_ListeningSkill_ActivityA.mp3 | 131 | U07_Pronunciation_Examples.mp3 |
| 47 | U03_Grammar_ActivityA.mp3 | 131 | U07_Pronunciation_ActivityA.mp3 |
| 48 | U03_UnitAssignment.mp3 | 132 | U07_SpeakingSkill_Examples.mp3 |
| | | 132 | U07_SpeakingSkill_ActivityA.mp3 |
| 52 | U04_Q_Classroom.mp3 | | |
| 54 | U04_NoteTakingSkill_ActivityA.mp3 | 137 | U08_Q_Classroom.mp3 |
| 57 | U04_Listening_ActivityA.mp3 | 138 | U08_NoteTakingSkill_ActivityA.mp3 |
| 57 | U04_Listening_ActivityB.mp3 | 140 | U08_Listening1_ActivityA.mp3 |
| 64 | U04_Pronunciation_Examples.mp3 | 141 | U08_Listening1_ActivityB.mp3 |
| 65 | U04_Pronunciation_ActivityA.mp3 | 141 | U08_Listening1_ActivityD.mp3 |
| 66 | U04_SpeakingSkill_Examples.mp3 | 143 | U08_ListeningSkill_Examples.mp3 |
| 66 | U04_SpeakingSkill_ActivityA.mp3 | 143 | U08_ListeningSkill_ActivityA.mp3 |
| 67 | U04_UnitAssignment.mp3 | 143 | U08_ListeningSkill_ActivityB.mp3 |
| | | 146 | U08_Listening2_ActivityA.mp3 |
| | | 146 | U08_Listening2_ActivityB.mp3 |
| | | 147 | U08_Listening2_ActivityD.mp3 |
| | | 153 | U08_Pronunciation_Examples.mp3 |
| | | 154 | U08_Pronunciation_ActivityA.mp3 |

# AUTHORS AND CONSULTANTS

## Authors

**Kevin McClure** holds an M.A. in Applied Linguistics from the University of South Florida and has taught English in the United States, France, and Japan. In addition to his extensive teaching experience, he served as the Academic Director at the ELS Language Center in San Francisco for eight years. He developed both print and online ESL/EFL materials. His main interests are computer-aided language learning and teaching conversation management skills to low-level students.

**Mari Vargo** holds an M.A. in English from San Francisco State University. She has taught numerous ESL courses at the university level. She has also written textbooks and online course materials for a wide range of programs, including community colleges, universities, corporations, and primary and secondary schools.

## Series Consultants

### ONLINE INTEGRATION

**Chantal Hemmi** holds an Ed.D. TEFL and is a Japan-based teacher trainer and curriculum designer. Since leaving her position as Academic Director of the British Council in Tokyo, she has been teaching at the Center for Language Education and Research at Sophia University on an EAP/CLIL program offered for undergraduates. She delivers lectures and teacher trainings throughout Japan, Indonesia, and Malaysia.

### COMMUNICATIVE GRAMMAR

**Nancy Schoenfeld** holds an M.A. in TESOL from Biola University in La Mirada, California, and has been an English language instructor since 2000. She has taught ESL in California and Hawaii, and EFL in Thailand and Kuwait. She has also trained teachers in the United States and Indonesia. Her interests include teaching vocabulary, extensive reading, and student motivation. She is currently an English Language Instructor at Kuwait University.

### WRITING

**Marguerite Ann Snow** holds a Ph.D. in Applied Linguistics from UCLA. She teaches in the TESOL M.A. program in the Charter College of Education at California State University, Los Angeles. She was a Fulbright scholar in Hong Kong and Cyprus. In 2006, she received the President's Distinguished Professor award at Cal State, LA. She has trained EFL teachers in Algeria, Argentina, Brazil, Egypt, Libya, Morocco, Pakistan, Peru, Spain, and Turkey. She is the author/editor of publications in the areas of integrated content, English for academic purposes, and standards for English teaching and learning. She recently served as a co-editor of *Teaching English as a Second or Foreign Language* (4th ed.).

### VOCABULARY

**Cheryl Boyd Zimmerman** is a Professor at California State University, Fullerton. She specializes in second-language vocabulary acquisition, an area in which she is widely published. She teaches graduate courses on second-language acquisition, culture, vocabulary, and the fundamentals of TESOL and is a frequent invited speaker on topics related to vocabulary teaching and learning. She is the author of *Word Knowledge: A Vocabulary Teacher's Handbook* and Series Director of *Inside Reading, Inside Writing,* and *Inside Listening and Speaking,* all published by Oxford University Press.

### ASSESSMENT

**Lawrence J. Zwier** holds an M.A. in TESL from the University of Minnesota. He is currently the Associate Director for Curriculum Development at the English Language Center at Michigan State University in East Lansing. He has taught ESL/EFL in the United States, Saudi Arabia, Malaysia, Japan, and Singapore.

iQ ONLINE extends your learning beyond the classroom. This online content is specifically designed for you! *iQ Online* gives you flexible access to essential content.

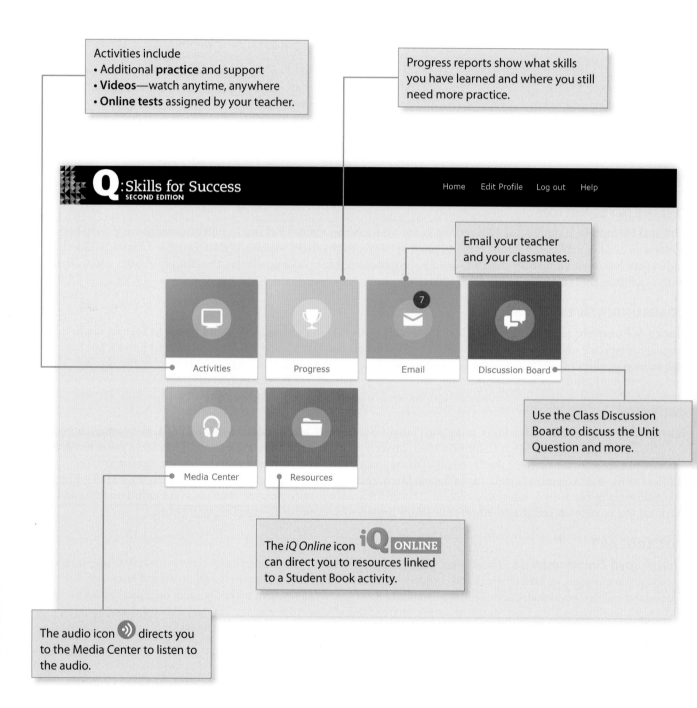

Activities include
- Additional **practice** and support
- **Videos**—watch anytime, anywhere
- **Online tests** assigned by your teacher.

Progress reports show what skills you have learned and where you still need more practice.

Email your teacher and your classmates.

Use the Class Discussion Board to discuss the Unit Question and more.

The *iQ Online* icon can direct you to resources linked to a Student Book activity.

The audio icon directs you to the Media Center to listen to the audio.

**SEE THE INSIDE FRONT COVER FOR HOW TO REGISTER FOR *iQ ONLINE* FOR THE FIRST TIME.**

## Take Control of Your Learning

You have the choice of where and how you complete the activities. Access your activities and view your progress at any time.

Your teacher may

- assign *iQ Online* as homework,
- do the activities with you in class, or
- let you complete the activities at a pace that is right for you.

*iQ Online* makes it easy to access everything you need.

## Set Clear Goals

**STEP 1** If it is your first time, look through the site. See what learning opportunities are available.

**STEP 2** The Student Book provides the framework and purpose for each online activity. Before going online, notice the goal of the exercises you are going to do.

**STEP 3** Stay on top of your work, following the teacher's instructions.

**STEP 4** Use *iQ Online* for review. You can use the materials any time. It is easy for you to do follow-up activities when you have missed a class or want to review.

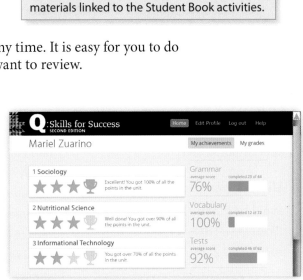

Notice the icon. It directs you to the online materials linked to the Student Book activities.

## Manage Your Progress

The activities in *iQ Online* are designed for you to work independently. You can become a confident learner by monitoring your progress and reviewing the activities at your own pace. You may already be used to working online, but if you are not, go to your teacher for guidance.

Check 'View Reports' to monitor your progress. The reports let you track your own progress at a glance. Think about your own performance and set new goals that are right for you, following the teacher's instructions.

*iQ Online* is a research-based solution specifically designed for English language learners that extends learning beyond the classroom. I hope these steps help you make the most of this essential content.

*C. n. Hemm*

Chantal Hemmi, EdD TEFL
Center for Language Education and Research
Sophia University, Japan

🔑 The keywords of the **Oxford 2000** have been carefully selected by a group of language experts and experienced teachers as the words which should receive priority in vocabulary study because of their importance and usefulness.

**AWL** **The Academic Word List** is the most principled and widely accepted list of academic words. Averil Coxhead gathered information from academic materials across the academic disciplines to create this word list.

**The Common European Framework of Reference for Languages (CEFR)** provides a basic description of what language learners have to do to use language effectively. The system contains 6 reference levels: **A1, A2, B1, B2, C1, C2**. CEFR leveling provided by the Word Family Framework, created by Richard West and published by the British Council. http://www.learnenglish.org.uk/wff/

## UNIT 1

belong to *(v.)* 🔑, **A2**
club *(n.)* 🔑, **A1**
collect *(v.)* 🔑, **A1**
good at *(phr.)* 🔑, **A1**
interested in *(phr.)* 🔑, **A2**
team *(n.)* 🔑 AWL, **A1**

## UNIT 2

active *(adj.)* 🔑, **A1**
community *(n.)* 🔑 AWL, **A1**
foreign language *(n.)* 🔑, **A1**
Internet *(n.)* 🔑, **A1**
skill *(n.)* 🔑, **A1**
special *(adj.)* 🔑, **A1**

## UNIT 3

avoid *(v.)* 🔑, **A1**
flavor *(n.)* 🔑, **B1**
social *(adj.)* 🔑, **A1**

## UNIT 4

exhibition *(n.)* AWL, **A2**
modern *(adj.)* 🔑, **A1**
nature *(n.)* 🔑, **A1**
path *(n.)* 🔑, **A1**
relaxing *(adj.)* 🔑 AWL, **B1**

## UNIT 5

comfortable *(adj.)* 🔑, **A2**
condition *(n.)* 🔑, **A1**
demand *(n.)* 🔑, **A1**
entertainment *(n.)* 🔑, **B1**
increase *(v.)* 🔑, **A1**
location *(n.)* AWL, **A2**
noisy *(adj.)* 🔑, **A2**
private *(adj.)* 🔑, **A1**
rent *(n.)* 🔑, **A2**

## UNIT 6

at least *(adv.)* 🔑, **A2**
energy *(n.)* 🔑 AWL, **A1**
habit *(n.)* 🔑, **B1**
lonely *(adj.)* 🔑, **B1**
manage *(v.)* 🔑, **A1**
prepare *(v.)* 🔑, **A1**
reduce *(v.)* 🔑, **A1**
regularly *(adv.)* 🔑, **A1**
stress *(n.)* 🔑 AWL, **A2**

## UNIT 7

average *(adj.)* 🔑, **A2**
climate *(n.)* 🔑, **B1**
create *(v.)* 🔑 AWL, **A1**
culture *(n.)* 🔑 AWL, **A1**
improve *(v.)* 🔑, **A1**

lecture *(n.)* AWL, **B1**
opportunity *(n.)* 🔑, **A1**
recently *(adv.)* 🔑, **A1**
resident *(n.)* AWL, **A2**
sight *(n.)* 🔑, **B1**
variety *(n.)* 🔑, **A1**
view *(n)* 🔑, **A1**

## UNIT 8

die *(v.)* 🔑, **A1**
discover *(v.)* 🔑, **A1**
distance *(n.)* 🔑, **A1**
government *(n.)* 🔑, **A1**
literature *(n.)* 🔑, **A2**
novel *(n.)* 🔑, **A2**
politics *(n.)* 🔑, **A1**
star *(n.)* 🔑, **A1**
universe *(n.)* 🔑, **B1**